PUBLISHER COMMENTARY

There is a reason the U.S. Air Force has one of the best cyberwarfare weapon system programs. This book pulls together 5 key Air Force publications on Cyberspace Defense Analysis (CDA), Risk Management Framework (RMF), and Information Dominance and Management.

AFI 17-2CDA, VOL. 1	CYBERSPACE DEFENSE ANALYSIS (CDA) TRAINING	7 Jun 2017
AFI 17-2CDA, VOL. 2	AIR FORCE CYBERSPACE DEFENSE ANALYSIS (CDA) STANDARDIZATION AND EVALUATION	7 Jun 2017
AFI 17-2CDA, VOL. 3	AIR FORCE CYBERSPACE DEFENSE ANALYSIS (CDA) OPERATIONS AND PROCEDURES	9 Jun 2017
AFM 17-101	RISK MANAGEMENT FRAMEWORK (RMF) FOR AIR FORCE INFORMATION TECHNOLOGY (IT)	2 Feb 2017
AFPD 17-1	INFORMATION DOMINANCE GOVERNANCE AND MANAGEMENT	12 Apr 2016

These publications cover guidelines for planning and conducting cyberspace operations to support the warfighter and achieve national security objectives. AFI 17-2CDA outlines Initial Qualification Training (IQT) requirements for all crewmember personnel, Mission Qualification Training (MQT) and Upgrade and Specialized Training as well as Continuation Training. It provides procedures, evaluation and grading criteria used during performance evaluations on operational cyberspace weapon systems. It provides governing directives and prescribes procedures for operating the CDA weapon system.

AFM 17-101 provides implementation instructions for the Risk Management Framework (RMF) methodology for Air Force Information Technology according to AFPD 17-1, and AFI 17-130.

AFPD 17-1 provides a means by which the AF will cross-functionally align cyberspace programs and capabilities to effectively and efficiently deliver capabilities to users. Cyberspace is defined as a global domain within the information environment consisting of the interdependent network of IT infrastructures and resident data, including the Internet, telecommunications networks, computer systems, and embedded processors and controllers.

Why buy a book you can download for free? We print this so you don't have to.

When a new standard is released, an engineer prints it out, punches holes and puts it in a 3-ring binder. While this is not a big deal for a 5 or 10-page document, many cyber documents are over 100 pages and printing a large document is a time-consuming effort. So, an engineer that's paid $75 an hour is spending hours simply printing out the tools needed to do the job. That's time that could be better spent doing engineering. We publish these documents so engineers can focus on what they were hired to do – engineering.

A list of **Cybersecurity Standards** we publish is attached at the end of this document.

BY ORDER OF THE SECRETARY
OF THE AIR FORCE

AIR FORCE INSTRUCTION 17-2CDA
VOLUME 1

7 JUNE 2017

Cyberspace Operations

CYBERSPACE DEFENSE
ANALYSIS (CDA) TRAINING

COMPLIANCE WITH THIS PUBLICATION IS MANDATORY

ACCESSIBILITY: Publications and forms are available on the Publishing website at www.e-Publishing.af.mil for downloading or ordering

RELEASABILITY: There are no releasability restrictions on this publication

OPR: AF/A3CX/A6CX

Certified by: AF/A3C/A6C
(Col Charlie Cornelius)
Pages: 41

This instruction implements Air Force (AF) Policy Directive (AFPD) 17-2, *Cyberspace Operations* and references AF Instruction (AFI) 17-202, Volume 1, *Cybercrew Training*. It establishes the minimum AF standards for training and qualifying/certifying personnel for performing crewmember duties on the Cyberspace Defense Analysis (CDA) weapon system. This publication applies to all military and civilian AF personnel, members of the AF Reserve Command (AFRC), Air National Guard (ANG), third-party governmental employee and contractor support personnel in accordance with (IAW) appropriate provisions contained in memoranda support agreements and AF contracts. The authorities to waive wing/unit level requirements in this publication are identified with a Tier ("T-0, T-1, T-2, T-3") number following the compliance statement. See AFI 33-360, *Publications and Forms Management*, Table 1.1 for a description of the authorities associated with the Tier numbers. Submit requests for waivers through the chain of command to the appropriate Tier waiver approval authority, or alternately, to the Publication OPR for non-tiered compliance items. This instruction requires collecting and maintaining information protected by the Privacy Act of 1974 (5 U.S.C. 552a). System of Records Notices F036 AF PC C, Military Personnel Records System, and OPM/GOVT-1, General Personnel Records, apply. Units may supplement this instruction. All supplements will be coordinated through HQ AFSPC/A2/3/6T prior to publication. Process supplements as shown in AFI 33-360. Major Command (MAJCOM) supplements will be coordinated with USAF A3C/A6C. Guidance provided by the lead major command will contain specific training requirements unique to individual and crew positions. Send recommended changes or comments to HQ USAF/A3C/A6C, 1480 Air Force Pentagon, Washington, DC 20330-1480, through appropriate channels, using AF Form 847, *Recommendation for Change of*

Publication. When collecting and maintaining information protect it by the Privacy Act of 1974 authorized by 10 U.S.C. 8013. Ensure that all records created as a result of processes prescribed in this publication are maintained in accordance with AF Manual (AFMAN) 33-363, *Management of Records*, and disposed of in accordance with the AF Records Disposition Schedule (RDS).

Chapter 1

GENERAL GUIDANCE

1.1. General. This instruction prescribes basic instruction and guidance for training United States Air Force Cyberspace Defense Analysis (CDA) crewmembers according to AFI 17-202 Volume 1, *Cybercrew Training* (T-2). Training instruction, guidance, and requirements are set forth for each phase of crew training. The objective of training should be the progressive development of CDA crew readiness.

1.2. Training Objectives.

1.2.1. The overall objective of the CDA training program is to develop and maintain a high state of readiness for the immediate and effective employment of the weapon system across a full range of tasked missions. Mission readiness and effective employment are achieved through the development and mastery of core competencies for CDA crewmembers. These core capabilities include monitoring voice, radio frequency communications, email, and Internet based capability for operational vulnerabilities.

1.2.2. The secondary objective is to standardize CDA training requirements within a single source document.

1.3. Abbreviations, Acronyms and Terms. See Attachment 1.

1.3.1. For the purposes of this instruction, "certification" denotes a commander's action, whereas qualification denotes a formal Standardization and Evaluation (Stan/Eval).

1.3.2. Key words explained.

1.3.2.1. "Will" or "shall" indicates a mandatory requirement.

1.3.2.2. "Should" indicates a preferred, but not mandatory, method of accomplishment.

1.3.2.3. "May" indicates an acceptable or suggested means of accomplishment.

1.3.2.4. "Note" indicates operating procedures, techniques, etc., which are considered essential to emphasize.

1.3.2.5. Note: The term "squadron" includes Air Reserve Components (ARC) "flight" components.

1.4. Responsibilities:

1.4.1. Lead Command. Air Force Space Command (AFSPC) is lead command for the CDA weapon system. The lead command is responsible for establishing and standardizing crewmember training requirements in coordination with user commands. AFSPC/A2/3/6 is authorized to manage all training course requirements and training tasks. AFSPC/A2/3/6 is the OPR for this AFI; AFSPC/A2/3/6 will **(T-2)**:

1.4.1.1. Chair a Realistic Training Review Board (RTRB) to review unit training requirements and programs. RTRB participants will include applicable AFSPC active and reserve component representatives. All units with assigned CDA crewmembers will be invited to send representatives and inputs. **(T-2)**

1.4.1.2. Process all change requests. **(T-2)**

1.4.1.3. Publish the annual Ready Task Memorandum (RTM). **(T-2)**

1.4.2. Wings and groups will:

1.4.2.1. Develop programs to ensure training objectives are met. Assist subordinate units in management of training programs, ensure programs meet unit needs, and provide the necessary staff support. **(T-2)**

1.4.2.2. Attach Crewmember Position Indicator (CPI) 1/6/8/A/Z personnel to an operational squadron. **(T-2)**

1.4.2.3. Except when otherwise mandated, designate the training level to which each CPI 1/6/8/A/Z will train. Upon request, provide AFSPC/A2/3/6T (through MAJCOM/A3T or equivalent) with a list of Mission Ready (MR) and Basic Mission Capable (BMC) individuals. Review programs and manning position designations annually. **(T-2)**

1.4.2.4. Develop additional training requirements and/or programs as necessary to meet unit mission requirements **(T-2)**

1.4.3. Squadron commanders. Squadron commanders will ensure at a minium, the following **(T-3)**:

1.4.3.1. Appoint an office of primary responsibility to manage and monitor the unit Ready Cybercrew Program (RCP). **(T-3)**

1.4.3.2. Train all designated crewmembers to MR. **(T-3)**

1.4.3.3. Operations training is responsible for maintaining training forms and unit certification documents for all unit personnel and personnel attached to the unit for mission purposes.

1.4.3.4. Adequate continuity and supervision of individual training needs, experience and proficiencies of assigned and attached crewmembers. **(T-3)**

1.4.3.5. Review of training and evaluation records of newly assigned crewmembers and those completing formal training to determine the training required for them to achieve MR or BMC status and to ensure provisions of this volume are met. **(T-3)**

1.4.3.6. RCP missions are oriented towards maintaining mission ready proficiency through tactical employment. Provide guidance to ensure only effective RCP missions are logged. **(T-3)**

1.4.3.7. Determine missions and events in which individual MR/BMC crewmembers will maintain qualification. **(T-3)**

1.4.3.8. Determine utilization of BMC crewmember. **(T-3)**

1.4.3.9. Determine special certifications and qualifications (if utilized). **(T-3)**

1.4.3.10. Assist the wing or group in the development of the unit training programs. **(T-3)**

1.4.3.11. Monitor assigned and attached crewmember currencies, proficiencies, and requirements. **(T-3)**

1.4.3.12. Ensure crewmembers participate only in sorties, missions, events, and tasks for which they are qualified/certified and adequately prepared, trained, and current. **(T-3)**

1.4.3.13. Ensure flight commanders or designated representatives monitor quality of training, identify training deficiencies, and advise SQ/CC or SQ/DO of additional training needs. **(T-3)**

1.4.4. Individual crewmembers will:

1.4.4.1. Be responsible for monitoring and completing all training requirements. **(T-3)**

1.4.4.2. Ensure they participate only in activities for which they are qualified/certified, current, and prepared. **(T-3)**

1.5. Training. Crewmember training is designed to progress a crewmember from Initial Qualification Training (IQT), through Mission Qualification Training (MQT), to annual Continuation Training (CT). Requalification Training (RT), and Upgrade Training (UT), are additional training requirements for the CDA weapon system.

1.5.1. IQT. One or more courses covering system specific and/or positional specific training as a prerequisite to MQT.

1.5.2. MQT. MQT prepares an individual for a successful formal evaluation. This training focuses on completing training requirements not met at IQT, mastering local procedures, and increasing proficiency as needed. MQT ensures a smooth transition from IQT to MR status.

1.5.3. CT. Training that provides crew members with the volume, frequency, and mix of training necessary to maintain proficiency in the assigned position and at the designated certification/qualification level. This training is identified within the respective lead MAJCOM-provided guidance.

1.5.3.1. Ready Crewmember Program (RCP). RCP is the CT program designed to focus training on capabilities needed to accomplish a unit's core tasked missions, fulfill Designed Operational Capability (DOC) statement mission requirements, and/or provide focus on mission sets as determined by the SQ/CC. Upon completion of IQT and MQT, crews will have received training in all the basic unit missions. After MQT completion, crews will then be assigned to MR or BMC status within the unit and maintain appropriate level of proficiency. **(T-3)**

1.5.4. RT. RT is designed to provide the training necessary to requalify a crew member with an expired qualification evaluation or loss of currency exceeding 6 months (for currency items specified in Chapter 4). A crewmember member is considered unqualified upon loss of currency exceeding 6 months, expiration of their qualification evaluation, or completion of a qualification evaluation in a different weapon system (unless multiple qualification was approved prior to the evaluation), whichever occurs first. The duration of unqualified time is measured from the date the crewmember member became unqualified until the specific retraining start date. **(T-3)**

1.5.5. MR. A cybercrew member who satisfactorily completed IQT and MQT, and maintains certification, currency and proficiency in the command or unit operational mission is MR. Completion of IQT, MQT, and a formal Stan/Eval evaluation are minimal requirements. **(T-3)**

1.5.5.1. All CPI 1/2/A/Z designated positions, to include SQ/CC and SQ/DO positions, will maintain MR status. The OG/CC may designate other CPI positions not assigned to the squadron as MR. See Attachment 4 for CPI explanation and definitions. **(T-1)**

1.5.5.2. MR crewmembers will maintain currencies that affect MR status, accomplish all core designated training (missions and events), and all mission related training **(T-3)**.

1.5.6. BMC. A crewmember member who satisfactorily completed IQT and MQT, but is not in fully-certified MR status. The crewmember member must be able to attain MR status to meet operational taskings as specified in the applicable lead MAJCOM-provided guidance. This status is primarily for individuals in units that perform weapon system-specific operational support functions (i.e., formal training units, operational test and tactics development). **(T-3)**

1.5.6.1. All CDA crew positions not specifically designated as MR coded positions, are BMC coded. BMC status is normally assigned to crewmembers with the primary job of performing wing supervision or staff functions that directly support cyber operations (e.g.,wing staff, OSS personnel, etc.). Many of these crewmembers are required to provide additional capability, either in lieu of or in addition to, the personnel assigned to the operational squadrons. **(T-3)**

1.5.6.2. BMC individuals must be able to attain proficiency and, if required, certification/qualification in 30 days or less for those missions/events that they maintain familiarization only. **(T-3)**

1.5.6.3. BMC crewmember accomplish all mission related training designated by their attached SQ/CC. **(T-3)**

1.5.6.4. Regression to Non-MR/BMC (N-MR/N-BMC). Once MR/BMC status is awarded, failure to complete the required MR/BMC CT and/or evaluation requirements will result in regression to N-MR/N-BMC status. N-MR/N-BMC personnel will accomplish required training and evaluation and be upgraded to MR/BMC before performing operational duties. **(T-3)**

1.5.7. Specialized Training. Specialized training consists of training in special skills necessary to perform the unit's assigned mission. Specialized training includes specialized mission equipment training, etc., and CT to maintain proficiency in special capabilities. Specialized training is accomplished upon assignment to MR or BMC status. Unless otherwise specified, crewmembers in MR or BMC positions may hold special certifications/qualifications provided additional training requirements are accomplished. **(T-3)**

1.5.7.1. SQ/CCs will determine and assign crewmembers that will train for and maintain special mission certifications **(T-3)**.

1.6. Training Concepts and Policies:

1.6.1. Units will design training programs to achieve the highest degree of readiness consistent with safety and resource availability. Training must balance the need for realism against the expected threat, crew capabilities, and safety. This volume provides training guidelines and polices for use with operational procedures specified in applicable operational publications. **(T-3)**

1.6.2. Design training to achieve mission capability in squadron-tasked roles, maintain proficiency, and enhance mission accomplishment and safety. RCP training missions should emphasize either basic mission skills, or scenarios that reflect procedures and operations based on employment plans, location, current intelligence, and opposition capabilities. Use of procedures and actions applicable to mission scenarios are desired. **(T-3)**

1.6.2.1. Unless specifically directed, the SQ/CC determines the level of supervision necessary to accomplish the required training. If the mission objectives include introduction to tasks or instruction to correct discrepancies observed during a previous mission, an instructor is required. **(T-3)**

1.7. Experienced Crewmember Requirements. CDA/Analysts (CDA/A) are declared experienced IAW Table 1.1. **(T-3)**

Table 1.1. Experienced Crewmember Requirements.

Position	Declared Experienced (Hours)
CDA Analyst (CDA/A)	400
CDA Operations Controller (CDA/OC)	400 CDA/A plus 400 CDA/OC hours
SMQ - Web Risk Analysis (CDA-WRA)	200
SMQ - Deployable Voice Monitoring System (CDA-DVMS)	200
SMQ - Fidelis SCOUT (CDA-SCOUT)	200
SMQ - Radio Frequency (CDA-RF)	200

1.8. RCP Policy and Management:

1.8.1. The RCP training cycle coincides with the fiscal year and is executed IAW the RCP RTM. Each RCP status (i.e., MR/BMC) is defined by a total number of RCP missions, divided into mission types, plus specific qualifications and associated events as determined by HHQ guidance and unit commanders. **(T-3)**

1.8.2. The total number of RCP missions for MR/BMC is the primary factor for maintaining an individual's RCP status. Variations in mission types may be used as a basis for regression as directed by the SQ/CC. Certification in a mission is determined by the SQ/CC considering HHQ guidance and the individual's capabilities. **(T-3)**

1.8.3. An effective RCP training mission requires accomplishing a tactical mission profile or a building block type mission. Each mission requires successfully completing a majority of the events applicable to that sortie type, as determined by the SQ/CC and Attachment 2. **(T-3)**

1.8.4. Non-effective sorties are logged when a training sortie is planned and started, but a majority of valid training for that type of mission is not accomplished due to system malfunction, power failures, etc. It is essential that non-effective sorties are logged and reported appropriately. **(T-3)**

1.8.5. A unit commander may move an individual from BMC to MR based on operational needs. Progression from BMC to MR requires:

1.8.5.1. A 1-month look back at the MR mission rate. **(T-3)**

1.8.5.2. Current certification event and qualification in all core missions and events required at MR. **(T-3)**

1.8.5.3. Confirmation the progressed crewmember can complete the prorated number of mission and event requirements remaining at MR by the end of the training cycle. **(T-3)**

1.8.5.4. Completion of mission-related training, to include a current certification as applicable to the assigned unit's DOC statement **(T-3)**.

1.8.6. End of cycle training requirements are based on experience level, as outlined in paragraph 1.7, on the last day of the current training cycle. **(T-3)**

1.9. Training Mission Program Development:

1.9.1. RTM MR/BMC mission and event requirements apply to all MR and BMC crewmembers as well as those with special mission certifications/qualifications (see Attachment 2). The standard mission requirements listed in the RTM establish the minimum number of missions per training cycle for MR and BMC levels of training. The RTM takes precedence over this volume and may contain updated requirements, missions, events, or tasks not yet incorporated into Attachment 2. The RTM applies to all CDA crewmembers. **(T-3)**

1.10. Training Records and Reports:

1.10.1. Units will maintain crewmember records for individual training and evaluations IAW:

1.10.1.1. AFI 17-202 V1, *Cybercrew Training*

1.10.1.2. AFI 17-202 V2, *Cybercrew Standardization & Evaluation Program*

1.10.1.3. Any additional HHQ supplement to the volumes listed above.

1.10.2. Track the following information for all crewmembers (as applicable):

1.10.2.1. Mission-related training (e.g., tactics training, crew resource management training, etc.). **(T-3)**

1.10.2.2. Requirements and accomplishment of individual sorties, mission types, and events cumulatively for the training cycle. **(T-3)**

1.10.2.3. RCP mission requirements and accomplishment using 1-month and 3-month running totals for lookback commensurate with CT status (MR/BMC). **(T-3)**

1.10.2.3.1. One -1-month Sortie Lookback: Total individual RCP sorties tracked for a 30-day time period. This lookback is used to assess individual progress in achieving the Total Sorties (minimum) required for the 12-month training cycle. **(T-3)**

1.10.2.3.2. Three - 3-Month Sortie Lookback: Total individual RCP sorties tracked for a 90-day time period. This lookback is used to assess individual progress in achieving the total sorties (minimum) required for the 12-month training cycle. **(T-3)**

1.10.2.3.3. ARC (individuals not on orders) will use 3-month lookbacks. **(T-3)**

1.11. Crewmember Utilization Policy:

1.11.1. Commanders will ensure wing/group crewmembers (CPI 6) fill authorized positions IAW UMDs and that crewmember status is properly designated (see Attachment 4 for CPI explanation and definitions) (T-2). The overall objective is for crewmembers to perform mission-related duties. Supervisors may assign crewmembers to valid, short-term tasks (escort officer, operational review board (ORB), etc.), but must continually weigh the factors involved, such as level of crewmember tasking, proficiency, currency, and experience. For inexperienced crewmembers in the first year of their initial operational assignment, supervisors should limit non-crew duties to those related to unit mission activities. **(T-3)**

1.11.2. Use evaluators as instructors for any phase of training to capitalize on their expertise and experience. If an evaluator is an individual's primary (greater than half of the accomplished training) or recommending instructor, the same evaluator shall not administer the associated evaluation.

1.12. Sortie Allocation and Unit Manpower Guidance: (T-3)

1.12.1. In general, inexperienced crewmembers should receive priority over experienced crewmembers. **(T-3)**

1.12.2. The RTM defines the minimum sortie requirements for crewmembers per training cycle. **(T-3)**

1.13. Training on Operational Missions.
Unless specifically prohibited or restricted by weapons system operating procedures, specific theater operations order (OPORD), or specific higher-headquarter (HHQ) guidance, training on live missions is authorized. In order to maximize efficient utilization of training resources, units will take maximum advantage of opportunities to conduct appropriate CT items that may be conveniently suited to concurrent operational mission segments. **(T-3)**

1.14. In-Unit Training Time Limitations:

1.14.1. Comply with the time limitations in Table 1.2. Crewmembers entered in an in-unit training program leading to qualification, requalification, or certification will be dedicated to that training program on a full-time basis **(T-3)**.

1.14.2. Training time start date is the date when the first significant training event (a training event directly contributing to qualification, certification, or upgrade) has begun, or 45-days (90-days AFRC) after being attached or assigned to the unit following completion of the formal training school; whichever occurs first. Training time ends with the syllabus completion. **(T-3)**

1.14.3. Units will notify the OG/CC (or equivalent) in writing before the crewmember exceeds upgrade training time limits in Table 1.2. SQ/CC may extend listed training times up to 60 days (120 days AFRC) provided appropriate documentation is included in the Individual Qualification Folder (IQF). **(T-3)**

1.14.3.1. Include training difficulty, unit corrective action to resolve and prevent recurrence, and estimated completion date. **(T-3)**

Table 1.2. In-Unit Training Time Limitations Active Duty (Calendar Days).

Training	Analyst	Operations Controller	Notes
Mission Qualification Training	90	N/A	1
Upgrade Training	N/A	90	1
Requalification	45	45	1
Instructor Upgrade	45	45	1
BMC to MR	30	30	1, 2
Notes: 1. Training time begins with the first training event **(T-3)** 2. BMC crewmember must be able to attain MR status and, if required, certification / qualification in 30 days or less for those missions/events in which they maintain familiarization only **(T-3)**			

Table 1.3. In-Unit Training Time Limitations ARC (Calendar Days).

Training	Analyst	Operations Controller	Notes
Mission Qualification Training	130	N/A	1
Upgrade Training	N/A	130	1
Requalification	90	90	1
Instructor Upgrade	90	90	1
BMC to MR	30	30	1, 2,3
Notes: 1. Training time begins with the first training event 2. BMC crewmember must be able to attain MR status and, if required, certification / qualification in 30 days or less for those missions/events in which they maintain familiarization only **(T-3)** 3. For activated AFRC only **(T-3)**			

1.15. Periodic and End-of-Cycle Training Reports.

1.15.1. Periodic Reporting. Squadrons will submit a periodic training report to MAJCOM/A3TT by the 15th of every 4th month of the training cycle (if the 15th falls on a weekend/holiday, then by the next duty day). Reports will consist of a SQ/CC memo summarizing previous report results/issues, current training plan summary and significant shortfalls/limiting factors affecting training. **(T-3)**

1.16. Waiver Authority:

1.16.1. Waivers. Unless another approval authority is cited ("T-0, T-1, T-2, T-3"), waiver authority for this volume is the MAJCOM/A3 (or equivalent). Submit requests for waivers using AF Form 679, *Air Force Publication Compliance Item Waiver Request/Approval* through the chain of command to the appropriate Tier waiver approval authority.   If approved, waivers remain in effect for the life of the published guidance, unless the waiver authority specifies a shorter period of time, cancels in writing, or issues a change that alters the basis for the waiver.

1.16.2. With MAJCOM/A3 (or equivalent) approval, waiver authority for all requirements of the RTM is the OG/CC. Additional guidance may be provided in the memo. Unless specifically noted otherwise in the appropriate section, and also with MAJCOM/A3 (or equivalent) approval, the OG/CC may adjust individual requirements in Chapter 4 and Chapter 5, on a case-by-case basis, to accommodate variations in crewmember experience and performance. **(T-2)**

1.16.3. Formal School Training and Prerequisites. Any planned exception to a formal course syllabus (or prerequisite) requires a syllabus waiver. Submit waiver request through MAJCOM/A3T (or equivalent) to the waiver authority listed in the course syllabus. If required for units' designated mission, events waived or not accomplished at the formal school will be accomplished in-unit before assigning MR status. **(T-2)**

1.16.4. In-Unit Training Waiver. MAJCOM/A3T (or equivalent) is approval/waiver authority for in-unit training to include syllabus and prerequisite waivers. Before approval, review the appropriate syllabus and consider availability of formal instruction and requirements. All in-unit training will utilize formal courseware in accordance with AFI 17-202V1. MAJCOMs will coordinate with the FTU to arrange courseware delivery to the unit for in-unit training. **(T-2)**

1.16.5. Waiver authority for supplemental guidance will be as specified in the supplement and approved through higher level coordination authority. **(T-2)**

1.16.6. Units subordinate to a NAF will forward requests through the NAF/A3T (or equivalent) to the MAJCOM/A3T (or equivalent). Waivers from other than the MAJCOM/A3 (or equivalent) will include the appropriate MAJCOM/A3 (or equivalent) as an information addressee. **(T-2)**

Chapter 2

INITIAL QUALIFICATION TRAINING

2.1. General. This chapter outlines IQT requirements for all crew positions. IQT includes training normally conducted during formal syllabus courses at the FTU. IQT begins after initial skills training is completed (i.e., the AFSC-awarding courses) and will take place at the FTU. Formal training and a successful INIT QUAL meets the criteria for crewmembers to achieve Basic Cyber Qualification (BCQ) status.

2.2. Waivers. AFSPC/A2/3/6 is the approval authority for in-unit IQT waivers due to FTU non-availability for Active Duty (AD) units (T-2). AFRC is the waiver authority for AFSPC-gained AFRC units and will forward all waiver requests regarding FTU waivers through HQ/AFRC to AFSPC/A3 for review (T-2). Waivers will be accomplished IAW **chapter** 1.17 of this document.

2.3. Local Training. In circumstances, when FTU training is not available within a reasonable time period, local IQT may be performed at the unit IAW the provisions of this chapter. Local IQT will be conducted using appropriate formal training course syllabus and requirements. When local IQT is authorized, the gaining unit assumes responsibility for providing this training. **(T-2)**

2.3.1. Requests to conduct local IQT will include the following:

2.3.1.1. Justification for the local training in lieu of FTU training. **(T-2)**

2.3.1.2. Summary of individual's mission related experience, to include dates. **(T-2)**

2.3.1.3. Date training will begin and expected completion date. **(T-2)**

2.3.1.4. Requested exceptions to formal course syllabus, with rationale. **(T-3)**

2.3.1.5. Personnel in local IQT will be evaluated at a minimum, according to the same standards used by AFSPC FTU for the end of course QUAL evaluation. **(T-3)**

2.4. Mission Training:

2.4.1. Mission sequence and prerequisites will be IAW the appropriate formal course syllabus (unless waived). **(T-2)**

2.4.2. Training will be completed within the time specified by the syllabus. Failure to complete training within the specified time limit requires notification through channels to MAJCOM/A3 with crewmember member's name, rank, reason for delay, planned actions, and estimated completion date. **(T-3)**

2.4.3. Crewmembers in IQT will train under the appropriate supervision as annotated in the formal course syllabus until completing the appropriate evaluation IAW AF Instruction (AFI) 17-202, Volume 2, *Cybercrew Standardization and Evaluation Program* (AFI 17-202V2) and AFI 17-2CDAVolume 2, *Air Force Cyberspace Defense Analysis (CDA) Standardization and Evaluation* (AFI17-2CDAV2). **(T-3)**

2.4.4. The formal course syllabus mission objectives and tasks are the minimum IQT requirements. However, additional training events, based on student proficiency and background, may be incorporated into the IQT program with authorization. Additional training due to student non-progression may be added at the SQ/CC discretion within the constraints of the formal course syllabus. **(T-3)**

2.5. IQT for Senior Officers:

2.5.1. All senior officer training (colonel selectees and above) will be conducted at FTUs unless waived IAW AFI 17-202 V1. **(T-2)**

2.5.2. Senior officers must meet course entry prerequisites and will complete all syllabus requirements unless waived IAW AFI 17-202 V1. **(T-2)**

2.5.3. If senior officers are trained at the base to which they are assigned they will be considered in a formal training status for the duration of the course. Their duties will be delegated to appropriate CDs or CVs until training is completed. Waiver authority for this paragraph is MAJCOM/CC (submitted through MAJCOM/A3) **(T-2)**

Chapter 3

MISSION QUALIFICATION TRAINING

3.1. General. MQT is a unit-developed training program for IQT graduates required to upgrade to MR or BMC status – it also includes local unit indoctrination. Guidance in this chapter is provided to assist SQ/CCs in developing their MQT program. Unit MQT programs must have OG/CC approval prior to implementation **(T-1).** Squadrons are allowed to tailor their program for individual crewmembers, based on current qualifications (e.g., USAFWS graduate, instructor), certifications, experience, currency, documented performance, and formal training. Applicable portions of MQT will be used to create a re-qualification program for personnel who are in N-MR or N-BMC status. At the completion of upgrade training, and a successful evaluation, individuals achieve MR/BMC for the applicable crew position. **(T-3)**

3.1.1. Personnel in MQT may only perform primary crew position duties under the direct supervision of an instructor for that crew position. The instructor is responsible for all actions and data derived by the personnel in MQT under their supervision. **(T-3)**

3.2. MQT Timelines.

3.1.1. Individuals will begin MQT no later than 45 days (90 days for the Air Reserve Component) after reporting to a new duty station or unit, unless waived by the MAJCOM/A3T. MQT will be completed within 90 calendar days (180 days for MAJCOM-gained ARC units) starting from the individual's date of enrollment. Training is complete upon SQ/CC certification of MR/BMC status (subsequent to the successful completion of the MQT MSN qualification evaluation). Notify the MAJCOM/A3T (or equivalent) if training exceeds the 90-day time period or there is a delay beginning MQT (e.g., due to security clearance) that exceeds 45 days. **(T-3)**

3.2.1. For individuals completing in-unit IQT, the first MQT training event must be completed within 15 calendar days from the completion of IQT. Further extensions require MAJCOM approval. **(T-2)**

3.3. Initial Certification:

3.3.1. Initial MR certification must be completed within 45 days after completing MQT (recommended, but not required for BMC). Each individual will demonstrate to a formal board a satisfactory knowledge of the squadron's primary DOC statement missions. Board composition will be established by the SQ/CC. Desired composition is SQ/CC or SQ/DO (chairman), weapons, training, intelligence, and other mission-area expert representatives. **(T-3)**

3.4. Mission Qualification Training:

3.4.1. Objectives: Be familiar with local area requirements and procedures. Specific mission tasks: local area familiarization, emergency procedures, and other tasks as determined by the unit. **(T-3)**

3.4.2. MQT programs should use profiles typical of squadron missions. **(T-3)**

3.4.2.1. Mission sequence and prerequisites will be IAW the appropriate unit MQT course syllabus **(T-3).**

3.4.2.2. Individual events may be accomplished anytime during MQT, however all events will be accomplished prior to SQ/CC certification of MR/BMC status **(T-3)**.

3.4.3. Supervision. An instructor is required for all upgrade training missions. **(T-3)**

3.4.4. Minimum Sortie Requirements. The minimum sorties required in a local MQT program will be IAW the MQT course syllabus (not required if portions of the MQT program are used to recertify crewmembers that have regressed from MR to BMC). Reference the paragraphs below for further details and recommended sortie flows SQ/CCs may use to develop the unit's MQT program. **(T-3)**

3.4.5. Training will be completed within the time specified by the syllabus. Failure to complete within the specified time limit requires notification through channels to the MAJCOM/A3T or equiavalent with crewmember's name, rank, reason for delay, planned actions, and estimated completion date. **(T-3)**

3.4.6. Formal course syllabus mission objectives and tasks are minimum requirements for MQT. However, additional training events, based on student proficiency and background, may be incorporated into the MQT program with SQ/CC authorization. Additional training due to student non-progression is available within the constraints of the formal course syllabus and may be added at SQ/CC discretion. **(T-3)**

3.5. MQT for Senior Officers:

3.5.1. Senior officers must meet course entry prerequisites and will complete all syllabus requirements unless waived by the MAJCOM/A3 **(T-2)**.

3.5.2. Senior officers will be considered in a formal training status for the duration of the course. Their duties will be delegated to appropriate CDs or CVs until training is completed. Waiver authority for this paragraph is the MAJCOM/CC (submitted through the MAJCOM/A3) **(T-2)**.

Chapter 4

CONTINUATION TRAINING

4.1. General. This chapter establishes the minimum crewmember training requirements to maintain MR or BMC. The SQ/CC will ensure each crewmember receives sufficient training to maintain individual currency and proficiency. **(T-3)**

4.2. Crew Status. SQ/CCs will assign crewmembers a crew status using the following criteria **(T-3)**:

4.2.1. Mission Ready. A crewmember who satisfactorily completed IQT and MQT, and maintains qualification, certification, currency and proficiency in the command or unit operational mission. Following IQT, MQT is a formal training program used to qualify crewmembers in assigned crew positions to perform the unit mission. This training is required to achieve a basic level of competence in the unit's primary tasked missions and is a prerequisite for MR or BMC declaration.

4.2.2. Basic Mission Capable (BMC). The status of a crewmember who satisfactorily completed IQT and MQT to perform the unit's basic operational missions, but does not maintain MR status. Crewmember accomplishes training required to remain familiarized in all and may be qualified and proficient in some of the primary missions of their weapon system BMC requirements. These crewmembers may also maintain special mission qualification.

4.2.2.1. The crewmember shall be able to attain MR status to meet operational tasking within 30 days. **(T-3)**

4.2.2.2. The OG/CC may declare an assigned or attached crewmember MR for a portion of the unit's operational mission if all training requirements are met. The crewmember does not need to attain MR status unless directed by the OG/CC. **(T-3)**

4.2.2.3. BMC instructors and evaluators may log instructor or evaluator time for the portion of the mission for which they are current and qualified. **(T-3)**

4.2.3. MR and BMC crewmembers will accomplish and/or maintain RCP requirements, for their respective status, and the appropriate events in the RCP tables in this instruction and the RTM. **(T-3)**

4.3. Training Events/Tables. Standardized training events identifiers and descriptions are in Attachment 2. Units will add unit-specific events to include a description in their local training documents **(T-3)**.

4.3.1. Crediting Event Accomplishment. Credit events accomplished on training, operational missions and satisfactory evaluations or certifications toward RCP requirements and establish a subsequent due date. Use date of successful evaluation as the date of accomplishment for all formal course mission-related training events. A successful evaluation establishes a new current and qualified reference date for all accomplished events. For IQT or requalification training, events accomplished prior to the evaluation are not creditable for any crew position. In all cases, events successfully accomplished during the evaluation or certification are creditable toward the crew position. **(T-3)**

4.3.2. For an unsatisfactory evaluation, do not log CT requirements for those events graded U/Q3 (according to AFI 17-202V2) until re-qualified. **(T-3)**

4.3.3. Instructors and evaluators may credit no more than 50 percent of their total CT requirements while instructing or evaluating. **(T-3)**

4.4. Continuation Training Requirements. Completion and tracking of continuation training is ultimately the responsibility of the individual crewmember. Crewmembers should actively work with their supervisors, unit schedulers and training offices to ensure accomplishment of their continuation training requirements. Crewmembers attached to units are responsible for reporting accomplished training events to their attached unit. **(T-3)**

4.4.1. Mission-Related Training Events. Crewmembers will comply with requirements of Table 4.1. **(T-3)**

4.4.2. Weapons and Tactics Academic Training. Units will establish a weapons and tactics academic training program to satisfy MQT and CT requirements. Training is required annually during each training cycle. SQ/CCs will provide guidance to unit weapons shops to ensure all crewmembers are informed/reminded of new/current weapons, systems, and mission-specific TTPs. **(T-3)**

4.4.2.1. Academic instructors should be the Chief of Weapons and Tactics.

4.4.2.2. Instruction should include (as applicable), but is not limited to:

4.4.2.2.1. Applicable AF Tactics, Techniques, and Procedure (AFTTP) 3-1 & 3-3 series publications, AFI 17-2CDA Volume 3, and other documents pertaining to the execution of the unit's mission. **(T-3)**

4.4.2.2.2. Specialized training to support specific weapons, tactics, mission capabilities, rules of engagement (ROE), and other mission related activities. **(T-3)**

4.4.3. Risk Management (RM). Crewmember will participate in RM training once every training cycle (T-2). Briefings will include the concepts outlined in AFPAM 90-803, *Risk Management (RM) Guidelines and Tools*. RM training will be tracked. Failure to complete RM training will result in Non Mission Ready (NMR) status. **(T-3)**

4.5. Mission-Related Training:

4.5.1. Units will develop training covering areas pertinent to the mission as determined by the SQ/CC (T-1). Training accomplished during IQT may be credited towards this requirement. Incorporate appropriate portions of AFTTP 3-1.CDA and other mission-related documents. **(T-3)**

4.5.2. Mission-related training may be tailored to the individual's background, experience and local conditions. Current and available reference materials, such as AFTTP 3-1.CDA, other applicable AFTTP 3-1s and 3-3s, unit guides, and other available training material and programs, will be used as supporting materials to the maximum extent possible. **(T-3)**

Table 4.1. CDA Crewmember Mission-Related CT Requirements.

Code	Event	Position	Frequency	Notes
MRT001	Weapons & Tactics	All	365d	1, 3,
MRT002	Risk Management	All	18m	2, 3, 4
Notes:				
1. "d" is the maximum number of days between events.				
2. "m" is the maximum number of months between events.				
3. Crewmembers may not accomplish unsupervised crew duties until the delinquent event is accomplished or waived.				
4. Affects MR status				

4.5.3. Mission Training Events. Crewmembers will comply with requirements of the RCP Tasking Memorandum (RTM) for their respective position. Total sorties and events are minimums which ensure training to continually meet all DOC tasked requirements and may not be reduced except in proration/waiver. Unless otherwise stated the OG/CC is the waiver authority for all RCP requirements and for all provisions in **Chapter 4** and **Chapter 5** of this volume. Failure to accomplish events in these tables may lead to NMR status. **(T-3)**

4.6. Specialized Mission Training (SMT). Training in any special skills necessary to perform the unit's assigned mission not required by every crewmember. Specialized training consists of CT to maintain certification, currency, and proficiency in unit tasked special capabilities and missions. **(T-3)**

4.6.1. Specialized training/certifications are normally accomplished after a crewmember is assigned MR/BMC status and is normally in addition to MR/BMC requirements. (See **Chapter 5**) **(T-3)**

4.6.2. The SQ/CC will determine and assign crewmembers that train for and maintain special mission qualifications and certifications. **(T-3)**

4.7. Multiple Weapon System Qualification/Currency. See AFI 17-202 V1, AFI 17-202 V2, applicable HHQ guidance, and AFI 17-2 *CDA Volume 2, Air Force Cyberspace Defense Analysis (CDA) Standardization and Evaluation* (AFI 17-2 CDAV2) for multiple qualifications.

4.7.1. Multiple crew qualifications are not appropriate for senior wing supervisors. **(T-3)**

4.7.2. Multiple Requirements. Crewmembers will satisfy at least 50 percent of the sortie requirements in their primary weapon system. If MR, they will meet all RCP mission and event requirements of the primary weapon system **(T-3)**.

4.7.3. Multiple Currencies. Crewmembers will conduct a sortie at least once each 45 days in each weapon system. They will comply with all other currency requirements for each crew currencies. **(T-3)**

4.7.4. Multiple weapon system qualified individuals must complete training IAW approved syllabus for each weapon system. **(T-3)**

4.8. Currencies, Recurrencies and Requalification.

4.8.1. Currency. The RTM defines currency requirements for MR/BMC crewmembers. Crewmembers may not instruct, evaluate or perform any event in which they are not qualified and current unless under instructor supervision. Currency may be:

4.8.1.1. Maintained by accomplishing the event as a qualified crewmember provided member's currency has not expired. **(T-3)**

4.8.1.2. Established or updated by accomplishing the event as a crewmember under supervision of a current instructor. **(T-3)**

4.8.1.3. Events satisfactorily performed on any training mission, evaluation, or operation may be used to establish or update currency in that event. **(T-3)**

4.8.2. If an individual currency expires, thereby requiring recurrency, that mission or event may not be performed except for the purpose of regaining currency. Non-current events must be satisfied before the individual is considered certified/qualified (as applicable) to perform those events unsupervised. Loss of currencies affecting MR status will require regression to N-MR). **(T-3)**

4.9. Loss of Instructor Status and Requalification/Recurrency. Instructors may lose instructor status for the following:

4.9.1. They become noncurrent in a mission or event which causes removal from MR/BMC status and the SQ/CC deems loss of currency is of sufficient importance to require complete decertification (but not a complete loss of qualification). **(T-3)**

4.9.2.1. As long as the affected individual retains instructor qualification IAW AFI 17-202V2, recertification will be at the SQ/CC's discretion. **(T-3)**

4.9.2.2. If the SQ/CC does not elect to decertify the individual or if the individual becomes noncurrent in missions or events which do not require removal from MR/BMC status, instructor status may be retained, but the instructor will not instruct that mission or event until the required currency is regained. **(T-3)**

4.9.3. Crewmembers losing instructor currency must accomplish the following:

4.9.3.1. 61-180 Days. Instructor recurrency with another current/qualified instructor. **(T-3)**

4.9.3.2. Over 180 Days. Conduct an instructor evaluation and document IAW AFI 17-202V2, applicable HHQ guidance, and AFI 17-2 CDAV2. **(T-3)**

4.9.4. Instructor Lack of Ability. Instructors serve solely at the discretion of the SQ/CC. Instructors should exemplify a higher level of performance and present themselves as reliable and authoritative experts in their respective duty positions. Instructors exhibiting substandard performance should be reviewed for suitability of continued instructor duty. Instructors will be decertified if **(T-3)**:

4.9.4.1. Awarded a less than fully qualified grade in any area of the evaluation regardless of overall crew position qualification. **(T-3)**

4.9.4.2. Failure of a qualification. **(T-3)**

4.9.4.3. SQ/CC deems instructor is substandard, ineffective, or providing incorrect procedures, techniques, or policy guidance. **(T-3)**

4.9.4.4. Decertified instructors may regain instructor status by correcting applicable deficiency and completing the training and/or evaluation as specified by the SQ/CC. **(T-3)**

4.9.4.5. Instructors fail to maintain currency resulting in removal of MR/BMC status. If an instructor becomes N-MR/N-BMC, they cannot instruct in that position until all currency requirements are completed. **(T-3)**

4.10. Regression.

4.10.1. MR/BMC Regression for Failure to Meet Lookback. Only RCP training missions, evaluations, or operations sorties may be used for lookback. If the individual does not meet lookback requirements throughout the training cycle, SQ/CC should remove the crewmember from a MR/BMC status.

4.10.2. RCP is an integral part of CT for crewmembers because, when they exceed the time interval for any RCP event or task, they become non-MR or non-BMC and enter into a phased training status for the overdue event or task. The different levels of training required to regain MR or BMC status are based on the amount of time the crewmember is non-current. **(T-3)**

4.10.3. Failure to meet RCP requirements for any event (as calculated from the date the event was last accomplished) will result in loss of currency for the overdue event and regression to N-MR/N-BMC status for that crew position. Members failing to meet RCP requirements will be supervised by a qualified instructor until the delinquent RCP events are complete as outlined in Table 4.2. **(T-3)**

Table 4.2. RCP Non-Currency Requirements. (T-3).

Number of Days Since RCP Item Last Accomplished	Requirement to Regain Currency
Up to 90 Days	Complete delinquent RCP tasks with an instructor current and qualified in the same crew position to reclaim MR/BMC status.
91-180 Days	Complete SQ/CC approved recertification program (documented in the individual's training folder) to return the crewmember to MR/BMC standards. Upon completion of the recertification program, the MR/BMC crewmember must also meet the subsequent 1-month lookback requirement and take open/closed book exams IAW AFI 17-202V2 prior to reclaiming MR/BMC status. Open/closed book exams will be documented IAW AFI 17-202V2.
181+ Days	Reaccomplish SQ/CC-directed MQT program to include a formal MSN evaluation IAW AFI 17-202V2, applicable HHQ guidance, and AFI 17-2CDAV2.

4.10.4. Failed Evaluations or Commander Directed Downgrades. Crewmembers who fail a periodic evaluation or receive a commander directed downgrade are unqualified. Crewmembers will remain unqualified until successfully completing required corrective action, re-evaluation, and re-certification by the SQ/CC. **(T-3)**

4.11. End of Cycle Requirements. Crewmembers who fail to complete mission or event requirements by the end of training cycle may require additional training depending on the type and magnitude of the deficiency. Refer to paragraph 4.12 for proration guidance. In all cases, units will report training shortfalls to the OG/CC. **(T-3)**

4.11.1. Crewmembers failing to meet annual RCP events or minimum total sortie requirements may continue CT at MR/BMC as determined by lookback. The SQ/CC will determine if additional training is required. **(T-3)**

4.11.2. Failure to meet specific MR and BMC mission type requirements will result in one of the following:

4.11.2.1. Regression, if the SQ/CC determines the mission type deficiency is significant. To regain MR/BMC, the individual will complete all deficient mission types. These missions may also be counted toward the total requirements for the new training cycle. **(T-3)**

4.11.2.2. MR/BMC may be maintained if total RCP missions and lookback are maintained and the mission type deficiencies are deemed insignificant by the SQ/CC. The SQ/CC will determine if any additional training is required to address shortfalls. **(T-3)**

4.11.3. Failure to accomplish missions/events required for Special Mission capabilities or certifications/qualifications will result in loss of that certification/qualification. The SQ/CC will determine recertification requirements. Requalification requirements are IAW AFI 17-202V2 applicable HHQ guidance, and AFI 17-2CDAV2. **(T-3)**

4.12. Proration of Training.

4.12.1. Proration of End-of-Cycle Requirements. At the end of the training cycle the SQ/CC may prorate any training requirements precluded by the following events: initial arrival in squadron, emergency leave, non-mission TDYs (i.e., PME), exercises, or deployments. Ordinary annual leave will not be considered as non-availability. Other extenuating circumstances, as determined by the SQ/CC, that prevent crewmembers from mission duties for more than 15 consecutive days may be considered as non-availability for proration purposes. The following guidelines apply:

4.12.1.1. Proration will not be used to mask training or planning deficiencies. **(T-3)**

4.12.1.2. Proration is based on cumulative days of non-availability for mission duties in the training cycle. Use Table 4.3 to determine the number of months to be prorated based on each period of cumulative non-mission duty calendar days. **(T-3)**

4.12.1.3. If IQT or MQT is re-accomplished, a crewmember's training cycle will start over at a prorated share following completion of IQT/MQT. **(T-3)**

4.12.1.4. No requirement may be prorated below one. Prorated numbers resulting in fractions of less than 0.5 will be rounded to the next lower whole number (one or greater). **(T-3)**

4.12.1.5. Newly assigned individuals achieving MR/BMC after the 15th of the month are considered to be in CT on the first day of the following month for proration purposes. A prorated share of RCP missions must be completed in CT. **(T-3)**

4.12.1.6. A crewmember's last month on station prior to PCSing may be prorated provided one month's proration is not exceeded. Individuals PCSing may be considered MR for reporting purposes during a period of 60 days from date of last mission/sortie, or until loss of MR currency, port call date, or sign in at new duty station, whichever occurs first. **(T-3)**

4.12.1.7. Example: TSgt Jones was granted 17 days of emergency leave in January and attended NCOA in residence from March through April for 56 consecutive calendar days. The SQ/CC authorized a total of two months proration from her training cycle (two months for the 73 cumulative days of non-availability). **(T-3)**

Table 4.3. Proration Allowance.

CUMULATIVE DAYS OF NON-MISSION ACTIVITY	PRORATION ALLOWED (Months)
0 – 15	0
16 – 45	1
46 – 75	2
76 – 105	3
106 – 135	4
136 – 165	5
166 – 195	6
196 – 225	7
226 – 255	8
256 – 285	9
286 – 315	10
316 – 345	11
Over 345	12

4.12.2. Operational Missions. The following procedures are intended to provide flexibility in accomplishing the unit's CT program. Sorties conducted during these missions will be logged. These sorties count toward annual RCP requirements and will be used for lookback purposes. Operational missions and events may be used to update proficiency/currency requirements if they meet the criteria in Attachment 2. **(T-3)**

4.13. Regaining MR/BMC Status.

4.13.1. If MR/BMC status is lost due to failure to meet the end-of-cycle event requirements, re-certification/re-qualification is IAW paragraph 4.10. **(T-3)**

4.13.2. If MR/BMC status is lost due to failure to meet lookback IAW paragraph 4.10, the following applies (timing starts from the date the individual came off MR/BMC status):

4.13.2.1. Up to 90 Days. On the 91st day to the 180th day, the individual must complete a SQ/CC approved recertification program (documented in the individual's training folder) to return the crewmember to MR/BMC standards. Upon completion of the recertification program, the MR/BMC crewmember must also meet the subsequent 1-month lookback requirement prior to reclaiming MR/BMC status. The missions and events accomplished during the recertification program may be credited towards their total/type mission and event requirements for the training cycle as well as for their monthly mission requirement. In addition, all RCP event currencies must be regained. The SQ/CC will approve any other additional training prior to MR recertification. **(T-3)**

4.13.2.2. 91-180 Days.   Same as above, plus open/closed book qualification examinations (IAW AFI 17-202V2). Open/closed book exams will be documented IAW AFI 17-202V2 and AFI 17-2CDAV2. **(T-3)**

4.13.2.3. 181 Days and Beyond.   Reaccomplish a SQ/CC-directed MQT program to include a formal MSN evaluation IAW AFI 17-202V2, applicable HHQ guidance, and AFI 17-2CDAV2. **(T-3)**

Figure 4.1. Regression Flow Chart.

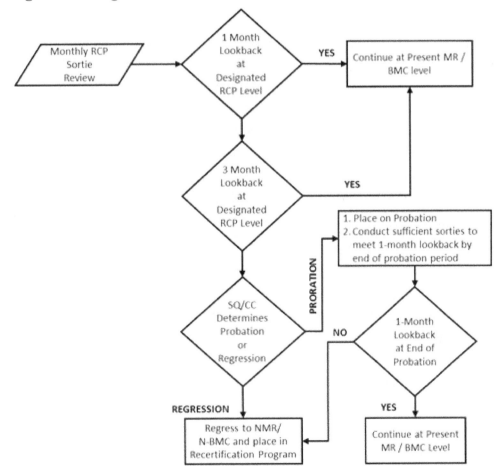

Chapter 5

UPGRADE AND SPECIALIZED MISSION TRAINING

5.1. General. This chapter outlines duties and responsibilities for units to upgrade, certify, and maintain currency/proficiency for special capabilities, and certifications/qualifications. SQ/CCs may tailor programs for individuals based on previous experience, qualifications, and documented performance. These capabilities and certifications/qualifications are in addition to unit core missions and do not apply to every crewmember assigned or attached to the unit.

5.2. Requirements. Requirements for upgrade and special mission training are listed in Table 5.1. Additionally, commanders must ensure each candidate has the ability, judgment, technical expertise, skill, and experience when selecting a crewmember for upgrade or specialized mission training. **(T-2)**

Table 5.1. Minimum Upgrade Training Requirements.

Upgrading From	Upgrading To	Prerequisites	Tasks & Events to Complete Upgrade
CDA Analyst	CDA Controller	Experienced Analyst	Controller task training Controller EVAL IAW 17-2CDAV2
CDA Analyst	CDA SMQ	Qualified Analyst	SMT, SMQ
CDA Operations Controller	CDA SMQ	Qualified Controller	SMT, SMQ
Any Position	Instructor	Experience minimum. Instructor Training Course	Instructor Qual SQ/CC certification INSTR EVAL

5.3. Instructor Upgrade. This section establishes the minimum guidelines for instructor upgrade.

5.3.1. An instructor will be a competent subject matter expert adept in the methodology of instruction. The instructor shall be proficient in evaluating, diagnosing, and critiquing student performance, identifying learning objectives and difficulties, and prescribing and conducting remedial instruction. The instructor must be able to conduct instruction in all training venues (e.g., classroom, training devices, ops floor, mission execution, etc.). **(T-3)**

5.3.1.1. Instructor Prerequisites. SQ/CCs will personally review each instructor candidate's qualifications to ensure the individual possesses skills necessary to upgrade to instructor. **(T-3)**

5.3.1.2. For instructor minimum requirements, see Table 5.2. All instructor candidates will be MR in their unit's mission. **(T-3)**

Table 5.2. Instructor Upgrade Requirements (T-3).

Upgrading From	Instructor	Tasks & Events to Complete Upgrade	Notes
CDA Operations Controller	100	Instructor Training Course Instructor Qualification Evaluation SQ/CC certification	See Note 1
CDA Analyst	200	Instructor Training Course Instructor Qualification Evaluation SQ/CC certification	See Note 1
CDA SMQ	200	Instructor Training Course Instructor Qualification Evaluation SQ/CC certification	See Note 1
Notes: 1. Training time begins with the first training event			

5.3.1.3. Training. Instructor training should expand the instructor candidate's weapon-system subject matter expertise. Instructor training will include methodology of instruction and make instructor candidates proficient in evaluating, diagnosing, and critiquing student performance, identifying learning objectives and difficulties, and prescribing and conducting remedial instruction. The instructor candidate must be able to conduct instruction in all training venues (e.g., classroom, training devices, ops floor, mission execution, etc.). **(T-3)**

5.3.1.4. Mission Execution. Instructor candidates will conduct a CDA mission via established planning and briefing, execution, and debriefing, (PBED) procedures through timely, accurate, and relevant integration, evaluation, and analysis of all available data, information, and intelligence. **(T-3)**

5.3.1.4.1. Locate mission essential information from previously executed missions and determine relevancy to current mission. **(T-3)**

5.3.1.4.2. Collect communications data and monitor/exploit raw communications data/activity and report IAW essential elements of information (EEI) for the area of interest. **(T-3)**

5.3.1.4.3. Maintain situational awareness of ongoing activity and account for all collected target(s)/activity during mission execution. **(T-3)**

5.3.1.4.4. Utilize applicable checklists as required. **(T-3)**

5.3.1.5. Testing. Units will develop tests based on the training requirements in AFI 17-202V1, HHQ Supplements, this publication, and other relevant guidance (T-2). Test will be closed book and consist of a minimum of 25 questions. To received credit for this training each instructor candidate must pass the test with a minimum score of 80 percent. Units will develop and maintain an instructor test master question file. Prior to the evaluation, instructor candidates will meet performance training standards IAW the CDA Instructor Upgrade course syllabus. **(T-3)**

5.3.1.6. Qualification and Certification. Instructor evaluations will be conducted IAW AFI 17-202V2and AFI 17-2 CDAV2 (T-2). The student is qualified to perform instructor duties after meeting all the criteria above, completing training, and a successful initial instructor evaluation. SQ/CC will certify a new instructor by placing a letter of certification in the training folder and indicate qualifications on a letter of Xs. **(T-3)**

5.4. Difference Training.

5.4.1. Difference Training (DT) is required for qualified and certified crewmembers when a new feature, variation, capability or procedure is initially introduced into the CDA weapon system, when an existing feature is introduced to a field site, or upon PCS or TDY to a new/different field site. **(T-3)**

5.4.1.1. Initial Introduction into CDA weapon system.

5.4.1.1.1. When a new feature, variation, capability or procedure is initially introduced to the weapon system, it requires new certification for each applicable crew position. The OG/CC will identify, and Wing/CC will approve the initial cadre, which is responsible to develop initial training materials **(T-1)**. Units will use these training materials to conduct difference training and award certifications to all applicable crew positions for successful mission execution. **(T-3)**

5.4.1.2. Existing Feature Introduced to a field site Location.

5.4.1.2.1. DT is required when an existing feature, variation, capability or procedure is introduced to a field site that didn't have it previously. That location will identify an initial cadre that will obtain training and training materials from a designated site operating with that feature. **(T-3)**

5.4.1.3. PCS/TDY to another field site.

5.4.1.3.1. Local area procedures for each field site may be different, and emergency area procedures for each field site will be different. When a qualified crewmember operates at another field site, that individual will require locally created DT prior to performing mission duties. Initial cadre is not necessary for this difference training type. **(T-3)**

5.4.2. DT may be incorporated into qualification and/or certification standards, as appropriate. **(T-3)**

5.4.3. Difference Training Timelines. Personnel that enter DT must accomplish the training within 60 calendar days (90 days for MAJCOM-gained AFRC and ANG units) from the date entered into training. **(T-3)**

5.4.4. Difference Training Documentation. All DT will be documented. **(T-3)**

WILLIAM J. BENDER, Lt Gen, USAF
Chief of Information Dominance and Chief
Information Officer

Attachment 1

GLOSSARY OF REFERENCES AND SUPPORTING INFORMATION

References

Privacy Act (5 U.S.C. § 552a)

AFI 17-202 Volume 1, *Cybercrew Training*, 2 Apr 2014, *Incorporating Change 1,* 6 May 2015

AFI 17-202 Volume 2, *Cybercrew Standardization and Evaluation Program*, 15 October 2014, *Incorporating Change 1,* 2 July 2015

AFI 17-2CDAVolume 2, *Air Force Cyberspace Defense Analysis (CDA) Standardization and Evaluation*

AFI 33-360, *Publications and Forms Management*, 1 December 2015

AFMAN 33-363, *Management of Records*, *Management of Records*, 1 March 2008, (*Incorporating Change 2*, 9 June 2016, *Certified Current* 21 July 2016).

AFPAM 90-803, *Risk Management (RM) Guidelines and Tools*, 11 February 2013

Adopted Forms

AF Form 679, *Air Force Publication Compliance Item Waiver Request/Approval*

AF Form 847, *Recommendation for Change of Publication*

Abbreviations and Acronyms

AF—Air Force

AFI—Air Force Instruction

AFMAN—Air Force Manual

AFPD—Air Force Policy Document

AFRC—Air Force Reserve Command

AFRIMS—Air Force Records Information Management System

AFSPC—Air Force Space Command

AFTTP—Air Force Tactics, Techniques and Procedures

AIM—Active Indicator Monitoring

ARC—Air Reserve Components

AFRC—Air Force Reserve Command

BCQ—Basic Cyber Qualified

BMC—Basic Mission Capable

CDA—Cyberspace Defense Analysis

CC—Commander

CMI—Classifed Message Incident

CORA—Cyberspace Operations Risk Assessment

CPI—Crewmember Position Indicator

CT—Continuation Training

CV—Vice Commander

CW—Cyberspace Wing

DO—Director of Operations

DOC—Designed Operational Capability

EEI—Elements of Information

EXP—Experienced

FLT—Flight

FTU—Formal Training Unit

HQ—Headquarters

HHQ—Higher Headquarters

IAW—In Accordance With

IDA—Information Damage Assessment

INEXP—Inexperienced

IPA—Information Protection Alerts

IQT—Initial Qualification Training

MAJCOM—Major Command

MS—Mission Supervisor

MISREP—Mission Report

MQT—Mission Qualification Training

MR—Mission Ready

MRT—Mission Readiness Training

NMR—Non Mission Ready

NVR—Network Vulnerability Report

OPORD—Operations Order

OPR—Office of Primary Responsibility

OSS—Operations Support Squadron

PBED—Planning, Briefing, Execution, and Debriefing

PCS—Permanent Change of Station

PII—Personally Identifiable Information

RDS—Records Disposition Schedule

RCP—Ready Cybercrew Program

RT—Requalification Training

RTRB—Realistic Training Review Board

ROE—Rules of Engagement

SCOUT—??????

SEPT—Situational Emergency Procedure Training

SMQ—Specialized Mission Qualification

SMT—Specialized Mission Training

SQ—Squadron

STAN/EVAL—Standardization and Evaluation

TDY—Temporary Duty

TRP—Training Review Panel

USAF—United States Air Force

USAFWS—United States Air Force Weapons School

UT—Upgrade Training

WG—Wing

WIC—Weapons Instructor Course

Terms

Basic Cyber Qualified (BCQ)—A crewmember who satisfactorily completed IQT. The crewmember will carry BCQ only until completion of MQT. BCQ crewmembers will not perform RCP-tasked events or sorties without instructor supervision.

Basic Mission Capable (BMC)—A crewmember who satisfactorily completed IQT and MQT to perform the unit's basic operational missions, but does not maintain MR status. The crewmember accomplishes training required to remain familiarized in all and may be qualified and proficient in some of the primary missions of their weapon system BMC requirements. These crewmembers may also maintain special mission qualification.

Certification—Designation of an individual by the certifying official (normally the SQ/CC) as having completed required training and being capable of performing a specific duty.

Continuation Training (CT)— Training which provides crewmembers with the volume, frequency, and mix of training necessary to maintain currency and proficiency in the assigned qualification level.

Currency—A measure of how frequently and/or recently a task is completed. Currency requirements should ensure the average crewmember maintains a minimum level of proficiency in a specific event.

Cybercrew Position Indicator (CPI)—Codes used to manage crewmember positions to ensure a high state of readiness is maintained with available resources.

Cyberspace Defense Analysis—Analyst (CDA/A) - This position's responsibilities include: process assigned data (Calls, Emails, IbC, and CORA); analyze data and assess impact to AF/DoD operations; notify the CDA/OC with flagged items, questions, concerns; identify and promptly report Classified Message Incidents (CMI)s and serious crimes and emergency situations; Information Protection Alerts (IPAs, immediate reports, Personally Identifiable Information (PII) Breach Reports, Network Vulnerability Reports (NVR), Summary Reports, Transcripts, CORA; develop pre- and post-mission briefings; create/modify Fidelis keyword searches; install Deployable Voice Monitoring System (DVMS) and Fidelis Scout; operate Fidelis, DVMS, and Fidelis Scout; and identify and report all system errors to the CDA/OC.

Cyberspace Defense Analysis—Operations Controller (CDA/OC) - In addition to the CDA/A responsibilities listed below, this position's responsibilities include: task each crewmember with Calls, Email/IbC, or Cyberspace Operational Risk Assessment (CORA) data to analyze; task or create mission brief or out-brief; manage frontline folder and determine if data meets reporting criteria; task or write Telephone Monitoring and CORA reports; task or create/modify Fidelis keyword searches; task or create phone line list; assist CDA/As with research, report write-ups, and identified disclosures; quality check analyst reports; monitor CDA/As for flagged items, questions, and concerns; notify the Mission Supervisor (MS) when reports are ready for final review; finalize and submit reports to the MD; purge alerts when authorized by the, MD; identify manning shortages and elevate to the MD; identify mission system problems/concerns and elevate to the MD; and immediately notify the MD of any emergency situations, serious crimes, or CMI.

Cyberspace Operations (CO)—The employment of cyberspace capabilities where the primary purpose is to achieve objectives in or through cyberspace.

Experienced Crewmember (EXP)—Experienced crewmember that meets the requirements in paragraph 1.7.

Mission—A set of tasks that lead to an objective, to include associated planning, brief, execution, and debrief. .

Mission Supervisor (MS)—In addition to the CDA/A and CDA/OC responsibilities, this position's responsibilities include: mitigate crew personnel shortages as identified by the CDA/OCs; monitor CDA/OCs for questions, concerns, accountability, etc; review and disseminate CDA reports and incidents; and review and distribute the Mission Reports (MISREPs). This posisition does not require a separate certification.

Mission Qualification Training (MQT)—Following IQT, MQT is a formal training program used to qualify crewmember members in assigned crew positions to perform the unit mission. This training is required to achieve a basic level of competence in unit's primary tasked missions and is a prerequisite for MR or BMC declaration.

Mission Ready—A crewmember who satisfactorily completed IQT and MQT, formal evaluation, and maintains certification, currency and proficiency in the command or unit operational mission.

Proficiency—Demonstrated ability to successfully accomplish tasked events safely and effectively. For purposes of this instruction, proficiency also requires currency in the event, if applicable. A crewmember is considered proficient when they can perform tasks at the minimum acceptable levels of speed, accuracy, and safety.

Qualification—Designation of an individual by the unit commander as having completed required training and evaluation and being capable of performing a specific duty.

Ready Cybercrew Program (RCP)—RCP is the formal continuation training (CT) program that provides the baseline for squadrons to develop a realistic training program meeting all DOC statement tasked requirements as well as specific NAF mission prioritization. RCP defines the minimum required mix of annual sorties, simulator missions, and training events crews must accomplish to sustain mission readiness. These programs have clearly defined objectives and minimum standards that enhance mission accomplishment and safety. RCP sorties are tracked. In order to be effective, each mission must successfully complete a sufficient number of events applicable to that mission type, as determined by the SQ/CC. With completion of IQT and MQT, a crewmember is trained in all the basic missions of a specific unit, unless a specific exception is provided in **Chapter 3** of the MDS-specific Vol 1. RCP applies to CMR/MR and BMC positions.

Sortie—The actions taken with an individual cyberspace weapon system to accomplish a mission and/or mission objective(s) within a defined start and stop period.

Special Mission Qualifications—Some MR and BMC crewmembers will carry additional qualifications in special missions. Unit CC/DO will determine which crewmembers will be qualified in special mission events. Unit CC/DO will determine if special mission events have affected C-rating and report variations through Status of Resources and Training Systems (SORTS). Special mission requirements are also shown in the RTM MR table.

Special Mission Training—Training in any special skills necessary to perform the unit's assigned missions that are not required by every crewmember. Specialized training is normally accomplished after the crewmember is assigned MR or BMC status, and is normally in addition to MR or BMC requirements. May be an additional certification or qualification event as determined by the unit commander.

Supervised Status—The status of a crewmember that must perform missions while being supervised by an instructor.

Supervisory Crewmember or Staff Member—Personnel in supervisory or staff positions (CPI 6 & 8) who actively conduct cyber operations.

Training Level—Assigned to individuals based on the continuation training status (basic cyber qualification, basic mission capable, or mission ready/combat mission ready) they are required to maintain.

Training Period—Any training period determined by the wing in which training requirements are performed.

Attachment 2

GLOSSARY OF MISSION, SORTIE AND EVENT DEFINITIONS

A2.1. Mission and Sortie Definitions: Applicable to Cyberspace Defense Analysis.

A2.1.1. CDA Primary Missions.

A2.1.1.1. **ESSA Mission:** The monitoring, collection, and analysis of information content transmitted across DOD electronic communication systems. ESSA products help evaluate an organization's OPSEC posture and determine the amount and type of information available to adversary collection entities. (Formerly the Telecommunications Monitoring and Assessment Program (TMAP). Protects information pertaining to Air Force, DOD and government operations, capabilities, and resources. ESSA missions identify and report disclosed information that could be used to compromise missions, gain access to sensitive capabilities, and deny knowledge of critical resources. ESSA utilizes the following tools: telephony, e-mail, IbC, radio frequency (RF), and web risk assessment (WRA). Authority is derived from DODI 8560.01, *Communications Security (COMSEC) Monitoring and Information Assurance (IA) Readiness Testing*.

A2.1.1.1.1. Telephony Communications: The monitoring and assessment of AF unclassified voice networks which if exploited by adversaries, can negatively impact AF operations.

A2.1.1.1.2. E-mail Communications: The monitoring and assessment of unclassified AF email traffic entering or exiting the AFIN which if exploited by adversaries, can negatively impact AF operations.

A2.1.1.1.3. IbC: (Internet Based Capabilities): The monitoring and assessment of unencrypted SMTP and HTTP communications that either enter or leave the AF Gateway architecture. **NOTE:** CDA units only "monitor" the web sessions that transverse the AFIN and not the IbC sites themselves. IbCs include collaborative tools such as social networking sites (SNS), social media, user-generated content, social software, e-mail, instant messaging, and discussion forums (e.g., YouTube, Facebook, Myspace, Twitter, Google Apps, etc.).

A2.1.1.1.4. Radio Frequency (RF) Communications: The monitoring and assessment of AF communications within the VHF, UHF, FM, HF, and SHF frequency bands (e.g., mobile phones, land mobile radios, wireless local area networks) which if exploited by adversaries, can negatively impact AF operations.

A2.1.1.1.5. WRA: The assessment of information posted on AF unclassified, owned, leased, or operated public and private web sites in order to minimize exploitation of AF information by adversaries that can negatively impact AF operations.

A2.1.2. **AIM Mission:** Identifies activities that potentially expose AF networks, systems and personnel to increased risk as a result of the action or inaction of an authorized user who discloses AF system credentials, accounts, exploitable network configuration information or PII. Protects the Air Force, DOD and government networks. AIM missions identify and report disclosed information that could be used to gain authorized access to compromise AF networks and devices. AIM tools include, but are not limed to e-mail and IbC.

A2.1.2.1. Telephony Communications: The monitoring and assessment of AF unclassified voice networks which if exploited by adversaries, can negatively impact AF operations.

A2.1.2.2. E-mail Communications: The monitoring and assessment of unclassified AF email traffic entering or exiting the AFIN which if exploited by adversaries, can negatively impact AF operations.

A2.1.2.3. IbC: (Internet Based Capabilities): The monitoring and assessment of unencrypted SMTP and HTTP communications that either enter or leave the AF Gateway architecture. **NOTE:** CDA units only "monitor" the web sessions that transverse the AFIN and not the IbC sites themselves. IbCs include collaborative tools such as social networking sites (SNS), social media, user-generated content, social software, e-mail, instant messaging, and discussion forums (e.g., YouTube, Facebook, Myspace, Twitter, Google Apps, etc.).

A2.1.2.4. Radio Frequency (RF) Communications: The monitoring and assessment of AF communications within the VHF, UHF, FM, HF, and SHF frequency bands (e.g., mobile phones, land mobile radios, wireless local area networks) which if exploited by adversaries, can negatively impact AF operations.

A2.1.2.5. WRA: The assessment of information posted on AF unclassified, owned, leased, or operated public and private web sites in order to minimize exploitation of AF information by adversaries that can negatively impact AF operations.

A2.1.3. **CORA Mission** : The analysis of compromised data from adversary exfiltration or friendly transmission outside of U.S. Government control, with the objective of determining the associated impact to Air Force operations and technology resulting from the data loss. CORA applies OPSEC principles and processes in the conduct of responsive and systematic analysis of the content of compromised data leaving the AFIN. While there are other similar capabilities analyzing compromised computers and networks, they are focused on methods, techniques, system vulnerability identification, and the identification or attribution of an adversary. CORA is a contributor to the overall Information Damage Assessment (IDA) process. It is focused on the nature and content of the compromised information itself, and the potential impact of its loss within the final IDA product. CORA capabilities assist information owners in determining the operational risk and impact of compromised information. Mitigates the effects of lost Air Force, DOD and government operations, capabilities, and resources. When conducting CORA missions CDA units are not monitoring or collecting any information from the AFIN. CORA is focused on the nature and content of the compromised information itself, and the potential impact of its loss within the final IDA product. CORA capabilities assist information owners in determining the operational risk and impact of compromised information. CORA utilizes the following tools: e-mail, IbC and Data at Rest. Authority is derived from AFI 10-1701, *Command and Control (C2) for Cyberspace Operations*.

A2.2. CDA Sortie and Event Definitions.

A2.2.1. If more than one primary/secondary/instructor/evaluator is on crew, each may obtain basic sortie credit if they actively participate in required pre-mission and post-mission procedures as described above.

A2.3. ESSA/AIM/CORA Sortie. Operational mission actions or training scenario profiles that relate to the unit's DOC statement requirements. Logged when performing real world ESSA, AIM or CORA. Credit this sortie for training or exercise missions when planned, briefed, executed, and debriefed to realistically simulate a typical operations mission. All training sorties will include a training scenario. ESSA/AIM/CORA sorties may be logged on actual real world operations missions or in a simulated environment that includes the standard crew configuration at minimum, appropriate pre-mission planning, all pre-mission preparations and briefings, and post-mission procedures. ESSA/AIM/CORA sorties require a minimum 1 MISREP in the operations controller duty position or while instructing/evaluating. An alert processing action and disclosure is required (all crew positions). Primary/instructor/evaluator time must be logged if performing the duties of instructor or evaluator. Missions designated to test weapon system capability/equipment may be logged as a ESSA/AIM/CORA sortie at the discretion of the SQ/DO.

A2.3.1. ESSA/AIM/CORA sorties may be accomplished either on the live system or in a simulator environment and must include (as a minimum) both and CDA/A and COC positions. A minimum of one hour of primary/instructor/evaluator time must be logged if performing the duties of instructor or evaluator. Sorties require system initialization with minimum status necessary for the crew to complete the pre-mission checklists. Minimum crew requirement may be waived by SQ/DO

A2.3.2. Training sorties should be designed to realistically train for the unit's operational mission, and will incorporate crew coordination between crewmembers, communication procedures, and system employment. Training sorties will be utilizied when real world situations are not practical. Training sorties can include (but are not limited to) new procedures, new hardware and software, profiency events, and primary missions.

A2.3.3. Commander Option. Sortie allocated by the unit commander to support individual training requirements and unit training objectives. BMC operators may log a Commander Option Mission for any type of mission listed in the "Missions required" table of the RTM.

A2.3.4. Instructor Sortie. Special qualification (see AFI 17-202V2). Sortie where the crewmember acted in an instructional capacity and valid operations training was secondary to execution of instructor duties.

A2.3.5. Non-effective Sortie. A sortie planned and launched as a training mission, test mission, Basic Skills sortie, or collateral sortie that, due to some circumstance (maintenance, etc.), fails to accomplish a sufficient number of planned events.

A2.4. RCP Events. RCP sorties are used for tracking profiency. Log an RCP event only when the event is accomplished.

A2.4.1. Disclosure Generation Event (DGE). Credit when accomplishing an actual or simulated alert processing event requiring proper alert analysis, crew coordination, and system operation resulting in a generated disclosure IAW published SOPs. Applies to both the analyst and controller.

A2.4.2. Network Vulnerability Report Event (NVRE). Credit when executed IAW local unit SOPs-can be baseline, topology, or credentials. Applies to both the analyst and controller.

A2.4.3. Personal Privacy Information Event (PPIE). Credit when executed IAW local unit SOPs. Applies to both the analyst and controller.

A2.4.4. Personal Identifying Information Event (PIIE). Credit when executed IAW local unit SOPs. Applies to both the analyst and controller.

A2.4.5. Information Protection Alert Event (IPAE). Credit when executed IAW local unit SOPs. Applies to both the analyst and controller.

A2.4.6. Immediate Report Event (IRE). Credit when executed IAW local unit SOPs. Applies to both the analyst and controller.

A2.4.7. Unique Report Event (URE). Credit when executed IAW local unit SOPs. Applies to both the analyst and controller.

A2.4.8. OPREP-3 Event (OPE). Credit when executed IAW local unit SOPs. Applies to both the analyst and controller.

A2.5. Mission-Related Training. Mission-related training is training required of all crewmembers as part of their CT program. Where conflict exists between this guidance and the RTM, the RTM takes precedence. Training accomplished during IQT/MQT may be credited toward CT requirements for the training cycle in which it was accomplished.

A2.5.1. **MRT001 Weapons and Tactics Training** .

A2.5.1.1. Purpose: Provide the crewmember with the information necessary for effective and successful execution of the unit's assigned mission.

A2.5.1.2. Description: MRT001 will be administered using courseware developed by the unit. The course will be based on AFTTP 3-1, AFTTP 3-3, AFI 17-2CDA V3 as well as other documents relevant to the execution of the unit's mission.

A2.5.1.3. OPR: Unit/DOK

A2.5.1.4. Course Developer: Unit/DOK

A2.5.1.5. Training Media: Lecture & Test

A2.5.1.6. Instructor Requirements: Academic instructors should be Chief of Weapons and Tactics (DOK) or DOK assigned tactician.

A2.5.1.7. Additional Information: Instructors teaching MRT001 may receive credit for their MRT001 requirement.

A2.5.2. **MRT002 Risk Management (RM) Training.**

A2.5.2.1. Purpose: Provide crewmembers with unit RM training according to AF Pamphlet 90-803, *Risk Management (RM) Guidelines and Tools*, other RM resources, and MAJCOM Supplements.

A2.5.2.2. Description: MRT002 will be administered using unit developed courseware. RM training introduces the common core RM subjects to provide crewmembers the information necessary to enhance mission effectiveness. Training should create a cultural mindset in which every crewmember is trained and motivated to manage risk and integrates RM into mission and activity planning processes ensuring decisions are based upon a risk assessment of the operation/activity. RM training will be tailored to meet the unique mission needs and operational requirements of each organization and to the personnel within the organization.

A2.5.2.3. OPR: Unit/DOK

A2.5.2.4. Course Developer: Unit/DOK

A2.5.2.5. Training Method: Lecture

A2.5.2.6. Additional Information: RM instructors teaching MRT002 may receive credit for their MRT002 requirement.

Attachment 3

CREWMEMBER RESOURCE MANAGEMENT (CPI)-1-6/-8/-B/-D

A3.1. Crewmember inventory requires close management at all levels to ensure a high state of readiness is maintained with available resources. To manage crewmember inventory, Crewmember Position Indicator (CPI) codes are assigned to identify these positions.

Table A3.1. Crewmember Position Indicator (CPI) Codes.

CPI Codes	Explanation	Remarks
1	Crewmember position used primarily for weapon system operations (Officer).	See Note 1
2	Crewmember position used primarily for weapon system operations (Government Civilians).	See Note 1
3	Staff or supervisory positions at wing level and below with responsibilities and duties requiring cyberspace operations expertise but which do not require the incumbents to operate the weapon system.	See Note 2
4	Staff or supervisory positions above the wing level with responsibilities and duties requiring cyberspace operations expertise but which do not require the incumbents to operate the weapon system.	See Note 2
6	Staff or supervisory positions at wing level and below with responsibilities and duties requiring the incumbents to actively perform cyberspace operational duties on the weapon system.	See Note 2
8	Staff or supervisory positions above the wing level with responsibilities and duties requiring the incumbent to actively conduct cyberspace operations on the weapon system.	See Note 2
A	Crewmember positions used for primarily for weapon system operations (Enlisted).	See Note 1
B	Staff or supervisory positions at wing level and below with responsibilities and duties requiring the incumbents to actively perform cyberspace operational duties on the weapon system.	See Note 2
C	Staff or supervisory positions at wing level and below with responsibilities and duties requiring cyberspace operations expertise but which do not require the incumbents to actively operate the weapon system.	See Note 2
D	Staff or supervisory positions above the wing level with responsibilities and duties requiring the incumbent to actively conduct cyberspace operations on a weapon system.	See Note 2
E	Staff or supervisory positions above the wing level with responsibilities and duties requiring cyberspace operations expertise but which do not require the incumbents to actively operate the weapon system.	See Note 2
Z	Crewmember positions used primarily for weapon system operations (Contractor).	See Note 1

Notes:
1. CPI-1, 2, A and Z are for officers, enlisted, government civilian, and contractor personnel assigned to operational squadrons or formal training programs. The primary duty of these personnel is to operate the weapon system to conduct cyberspace operations.
2. CPI-3, 4, 6, 8, B, C, D, and E identify crewmembers assigned to supervisory or staff positions. These positions require cyberspace operations experience with some requiring weapon system operation (CPI-6, 8, B, and D).

Attachment 4

TRAINING POLICY

A4.1. Training System/Station Not Capable of Operations. If a system/station is not capable of operations, the chief operations training, or staff instructor should either cancel the training sortie or devise an alternate course of action.

A4.2. Training/Evaluation Briefings. Before all training/evaluation missions, Crew Leads or instructors/flight examiners will brief their crews on the following additional items:

A4.2.1. Training/Evaluation requirements. Instructors/evaluators (for each crew position) will outline requirements and objectives for each trainee or examinee.

A4.2.2. Planned training profiles and seat changes.

A4.3. Debriefing. Review and evaluate overall training performed. Each trainee or crewmember should thoroughly understand the training accomplished. Ensure alltraining is documented.

BY ORDER OF THE SECRETARY *OF THE AIR FORCE*	*AIR FORCE INSTRUCTION 17-2CDA* *VOLUME 2*

7 JUNE 2017

Cyberspace

AIR FORCE CYBERSPACE DEFENSE
ANALYSIS (CDA) STANDARDIZATION
AND EVALUATION

COMPLIANCE WITH THIS PUBLICATION IS MANDATORY

ACCESSIBILITY: Publications and forms are available for downloading or ordering on the e- Publishing website at www.e-Publishing.af.mil

RELEASABILITY: There are no releasability restrictions on this publication

OPR: AF/A3CX/A6CX

Certified by: AF/A3C/A6C
(Col Charles Cornelius)
Pages: 29

This Instruction implements Air Force (AF) Policy Directive (AFPD) 17-2, *Cyberspace Operations* and references Air Force Instruction (AFI) 17-202 Volume 2, *Cybercrew Standardization and Evaluation Program*. It establishes the Crew Standardization and Evaluation (Stan/Eval) procedures and evaluation criteria for qualifying crew members in the Cyber Defense Analysis (CDA) weapon system. This publication applies to all military and civilian AF personnel, members of AF Reserve Command (AFRC) units and the Air National Guard (ANG). Refer to paragraph 1.3 for information on the authority to waive provisions of this AFI. This publication may be supplemented at the unit level, but all direct supplements must be routed through channels to HQ USAF/A3C/A6C for coordination prior to certification and approval. The authorities to waive wing/unit level requirements in this publication are identified with a Tier ("T-0, T-1, T-2, T-3") number following the compliance statement. See AFI 33-360, *Publications and Forms Management*, Table 1.1 for a description of the authorities associated with the Tier numbers. Submit requests for waivers through the chain of command to the appropriate Tier waiver approval authority, or alternately, to the Publication Office of Primary Responsibility (OPR) for non-tiered compliance items. Send recommended changes or comments to the OPR (HQ USAF/A3C/A6C, 1480 Air Force Pentagon, Washington, DC 20330-1480), using AF Form 847, *Recommendation for Change of Publication*; route AF Forms 847 from the field through the chain of command. This Instruction requires collecting and maintaining information protected by the Privacy Act of 1974 (5 U.S.C. 552a). System of records notices F036 AF PC C, Military Personnel Records System, and OPM/GOVT-1, General Personnel Records, apply. When collecting and maintaining information protect it by the Privacy

Act of 1974 authorized by 10 U.S.C. 8013. Ensure all records created as a result of processes prescribed in this publication are maintained in accordance with (IAW) AF Manual (AFMAN) 33-363, *Management of Records*, and disposed of in accordance with the AF Records Disposition Schedule (RDS).

Chapter 1

GENERAL INFORMATION

1.1. General. This instruction provides cyberspace operations examiners and cybercrew members with procedures and evaluation criteria used during performance evaluations on the CDA weapon system. For evaluation purposes, refer to this AFI for evaluation standards. Adherence to these procedures and criteria will ensure an accurate assessment of the proficiency and capabilities of cybercrew members. In addition to general criteria information and grading criteria, this AFI provides specific information and grading criteria for each crew position, special mission qualification (SMQ), instructor upgrade qualification, and Stan/Eval examiner objectivity evaluations.

1.2. Recommendation for Change of Publication. Recommendations for improvements to this volume will be submitted on AF Form 847, through the appropriate Functional chain of command to HQ USAF/A3CX/A6CX. Approved recommendations will be collated into interim or formal change notices, and forwarded to HQ 24 AF/A3T for HQ 24 AF/A3 approval.

1.3. Waivers. Unless another approval authority is cited ("T-0, T-1, T-2, T-3"), waiver authority for this volume is the MAJCOM/A3 (or equivalent). Submit requests for waivers using AF Form 679, *Air Force Publication Compliance Item Waiver Request/Approval*, through the chain of command to the appropriate Tier waiver approval authority. If approved, waivers remain in effect for the life of the published guidance, unless the waiver authority specifies a shorter period of time, cancels in writing, or issues a change that alters the basis for the waiver.

1.4. Procedures:

1.4.1. Standardization and Evaluation Examiners (SEEs) will use the grading policies in AFI 17-202V2 and the evaluation criteria in this instruction volume for conducting all AFSPC and AFSPC-oversight units' weapon system performance, Cybercrew Training Device (CTD), and Emergency Procedures Evaluations (EPE). All evaluations assume a stable platform and normal operating conditions. Compound emergency procedures (multiple simultaneous EPEs) will not be used.

1.4.2. Each squadron will design and maintain evaluation profiles for each mission/weapon system that includes information on each crew position. These profiles, approved by Operations Group Standardization/Evaluation (OGV), should outline the minimum number and type of events to be performed/observed to satisfy a complete evaluation. Evaluation profiles will incorporate requirements established in the applicable grading criteria and reflect the primary unit tasking. **(T-3)**

1.4.3. All evaluations fall under the categories listed in AFI 17-202V2. For dual/multiple qualification or difference evaluations that do not update an eligibility period, list as Spot Evaluation (SPOT) on the front of the AF Form 4418, *Certificate of Cybercrew Qualification*, and explain it was a difference evaluation under "Mission Description." **(T-3)**

1.4.3.1. Schedule all evaluation activity on one mission/sortie to the greatest extent possible. All performance phase requirements should be accomplished during a training (or operational if training not available) mission/sortie. If a required event is not accomplished during a mission/sortie, the event may be completed in the CTD. This may be delegated no lower than SQ/CC unless otherwise authorized in position specific chapters of this instruction volume. **(T-2)**

1.4.3.2. During all evaluations, any grading areas observed by the evaluator may be evaluated. If additional training is required for areas outside of the scheduled evaluation, document the training required under the appropriate area on the AF Form 4418. **(T-2)**

1.4.3.3. This AFI contains a table of requirements for the written requisites and a table for the grading criteria for various evaluations. Each table may include a "Note" which refers to a general note found in the individual grading criteria, and/or a number which refers to a note shown below the table. To complete an evaluation, all areas annotated with an "R" must be successfully completed. **(T-2)**

1.4.3.4. Unit examiners may administer evaluations outside of their organization to include evaluations between MAJCOMs, provided written agreements/understandings between the affected organizations are in-place. Written agreements/understandings shall be reviewed and updated annually. **(T-3)**

1.4.4. Cumulative deviations should be considered when determining the overall grade. The SEE will state the examinee's overall rating, review with the examinee the area grades assigned, thoroughly critique specific deviations, and recommend/assign any required additional training. **(T-3)**

1.4.5. SEEs will not evaluate students with whom they instructed 50% of the qualification/upgrade training or those they recommend for qualification/upgrade evaluation without SQ/CC approval. **(T-3)**

1.4.6. All crewmembers for the sortie (to include students, instructors, examinees, and evaluators) will participate in and adhere to all required mission planning, mission briefing, mission execution, and mission debriefing requirements. All crewmembers must be current on Crew Information File (CIF) and meet all Go/No-Go requirements IAW AFI 17-202 series instructions, this instruction, and all applicable supplemental guidance prior to operating, instructing, or evaluating on the weapon system. **(T-2)**

1.5. General Evaluation Requirements:

1.5.1. Publications Check. In units where crewmembers are individually issued technical orders, operating manuals, checklists, crew aids, etc., for use in conducting operations, a publications check will be accomplished for all evaluations. The publications check will be annotated in the comments block of the AF Form 4418 only if unsatisfactory. List of Effective Pages (LEP) and annual "A" page checks in individually issued operating manuals must be accomplished, documented, and current. OGV will list the minimum required operating publications each cybercrew member is responsible for in the unit CIF Library and/or unit supplement to AFI 17-202V2. NOTE: In units where such resources are not individually issued but made available/accessible for common use, the squadron Stan/Eval office will list those items (version and date) and ensure the accuracy and currency of the information contained in those. **(T-2)**

1.5.2. Written Examinations:

1.5.2.1. The requisites in Table 1.1 are common to all CDA crew positions and will be accomplished IAW AFI 17-202V2, all applicable supplemental guidance, and unit directives. These will be accomplished prior to the sortie performance phase unless in conjunction with an No Notice (N/N) Qualification (QUAL). NOTE: A N/N evaluation conducted in the examinee's eligibility period and meeting all required QUAL profile requirements affords the examinee to opt for the N/N evaluation to satisfy a periodic QUAL, in which case the examinee may complete written and Emergency Procedures Evaluations (EPE) requisites after the performance phase. However, the written examination(s) and EPE must be completed prior to the examinee's expiration date. **(T-2)**

1.5.3. Emergency Procedures Evaluations (EPE). Every Qualification evaluation which updates an expiration date will include an EPE. Qualification EPEs will evaluate the crewmember's knowledge and/or performance of emergency procedures, to include use of emergency equipment. Use the Emergency Procedures/Equipment grading criteria for all emergency situations. Use Systems Knowledge/Operations grading criteria to evaluate general systems operation. An EPE may be accomplished prior to the mission with any unit SEE conducting a scenario-based evaluation using question/answer (Q&A) techniques, preferably during the SEE pre-brief with the examinee. Units will determine scenarios for EPEs. The SEE will assign an overall EPE grade (1 or 3). Document the accomplishment and result of the EPE in the Written Phase block of Section II Qualification on the AF Form 4418. **(T-3)**

Table 1.1. Crew Position Specific Requirements - Written Examinations.

Examination Type	CDA-A QUAL	CDA-OC QUAL
OPEN BOOK (Note 1)	O	O
CLOSED BOOK (Note 2)	R	R
EPE	R	R
R – Required; O – Optional NOTES: 1. Units may administer OPEN BOOK exams at their discretion, however it is not required. If utilized, exams shall consist of a minimum of 40 questions derived from applicable operations manuals and governing directives. OG/OGV will determine the necessary number of questions to be included for each weapon system and crew position. **(T-3)** 2. The CLOSED BOOK exam consists of a minimum of 25 questions derived from applicable operations manuals and governing directives. OG/OGV will determine the necessary number of questions to be included for each weapon system and crew position. **(T-3)**		

1.5.4. Qualification (QUAL) Evaluations. These evaluations measure a crewmember's ability to meet grading areas listed on Table 1.2. at the end of this chapter and defined in **Chapter 2** of this instruction. IAW AFI 17-202V2 and lead MAJCOM guidance, QUAL evaluations may be combined with MSN evaluations. When practical, an individual's QUAL evaluation may be combined with their Instructor evaluation, as applicable for the crew position. **(T-2)**

1.5.5. Special Mission Qualification (SMQ) upgrade CLOSED BOOK exam is a separate closed book exam consisting of a minimum 25 questions specific to the SMQ derived from applicable operations manuals and governing directives. For initial SMQ evaluations that are not combined with the member's periodic QUAL (for the primary crew position), the SMQ exam is the only required exam. Subsequent (periodic) SMQ evaluations should be combined with the member's periodic QUAL evaluation, therefore, requiring the written requisites to consist of the applicable OPEN BOOK, CLOSED BOOK, and applicable SMQ exam(s). **(T-2)**

1.5.6. Mission (MSN) Evaluations. IAW AFI 17-202V2 and lead MAJCOM guidance, the requirement for a separate MSN evaluation may be combined with the QUAL evaluation. The various procedures and techniques used throughout the different weapon system variants are managed through a training program which results in a mission certification. Mission certifications will be IAW 17-202 Vol 1, AFI 17-2CDA Vol 1, and all applicable supplements and will be documented in the appropriate training folder. MSN and SMQ evaluation grading areas are also listed on Table 1.2. at the end of this chapter and defined in Chapter 2 of this instruction. **(T-2)**

1.5.6.1. For crewmembers who maintain multiple mission certifications, recurring evaluations need only evaluate the primary mission events as long as currency is maintained in all other required training events. **(T-2)**

1.5.7. Instructor Evaluations. Grading areas for these evaluations are listed on Table 1.2. at the end of this chapter. See Chapter 3 of this instruction for amplified information and grading area definitions. **(T-2)**

1.5.8. Stan/Eval Examiner (SEE) Objectivity Evaluations. Grading areas for these evaluations are listed on Table 1.2. at the end of this chapter. See Chapter 4 of this instruction for amplified information and grading area definitions. **(T-2)**

1.5.9. No-Notice Evaluations. OG/CC will determine no-notice evaluation procedures/goals. **(T-3)**

1.6. Grading Instructions. Standards and performance parameters are contained in AFI 17-202V2 and this instruction. A three-level grading system is used for most areas; however a "Q-" grade will not be indicated under critical areas. **(T-3)**

1.6.1. Critical Area/Subarea. Critical areas are events that require adequate accomplishment by the examinee to successfully and safely achieve the mission/sortie objectives and complete the evaluation. These events, if not adequately accomplished could result in mission failure, endanger human life, or cause serious injury or death. Additionally, critical areas/subareas apply to time-sensitive tasks or tasks that must be accomplished as expeditiously as possible without any intervening lower priority actions that would, in the normal sequence of events, adversely affect task performance/outcome. If an examinee receives a "U" grade in any critical area, the overall grade for the evaluation will be "Q3." Critical areas are identified by "(C)" following the applicable area title. **(T-2)**

1.6.2. Major Area/Subarea. Major areas are events or tasks deemed integral to the performance of other tasks and required to sustain acceptable weapon system operations and mission execution. If an examinee receives a "U" grade in a non-critical area then the overall grade awarded will be no higher than "Q2." An examinee receiving a "Q-" grade in a non-critical area or areas may still receive a "Q1" overall grade at evaluator discretion. An overall "Q3" can be awarded if, in the judgment of the flight examiner, there is justification based on performance in one or several areas/sub areas. **(T-2)**

1.6.3. The SEE must exercise judgment when the wording of areas is subjective and when specific situations are not covered. Evaluator judgment will be the final determining factor in deciding the overall qualification level. **(T-2)**

Table 1.2. Crew Position Specific Requirements - Performance Phase Evaluations. (T-3)

AREA/TITLE	Cat	Crew Positions		Special Mission Quals				Upgrade	
	C, M, m	CD A-A	CD A-OC	WRA	D V M S	SC OU T	R F	INST R	SE E
1. Situational Awareness	C	R	R						
2. Safety	C	R	R						
3. Crew Discipline	C	R	R						
4. Emergency Procedures/Equipment		R	R						
5. Mission Planning		R	R						
6. Briefing		R	R						
7. Pre-Mission Activity		R	R						
8. Mission Checks/Checklist Procedures		R	R						
9. Crew Coordination		R	R						
10. Task Management		R	R						
11. Communication		R	R						
12. Systems Knowledge/Operations		R	R						
13. Reports and Transcripts		R	R						
14. Emergency/Criminal Information Reporting	C	R	R						
15. Classified Message Incident Procedures	C	R	R						
16. Post-Mission Activity		R	R						
17. Debrief		R	R						
18. Mission Management			R						
19. WRA Collection and Analysis				R					
20. DVMS Collection and Analysis					R				
21. SCOUT Collection and Analysis						R			
22. RF Collection and Analysis							R		
Instructor Upgrade Evaluation Criteria									
23. Instructional Ability								R	
24. Instructional Briefings/Critique								R	
25. Demonstration and Performance								R	
SEE Objectivity Evaluation Criteria									
26. Compliance with Directives									R
27. SEE Briefing									R
38. Performance Assessment /Grading									R

29. Additional Training Assignment									R, 1
30. Examinee Debrief									R
31. Supervisor Debrief									R, 1
32. SEE Performance/Documentation									R
C – Critical; R – Required NOTES: 1. If required due to examinee's performance.									

Chapter 2

CREW POSITION EVALUATIONS AND GRADING CRITERIA

2.1. General. The grading criteria contained in this chapter are applicable to evaluations for CDA Operations Controllers (CDA-OC) and Analysts (CDA-A), and were established by experience, policies, and procedures set forth in weapon system manuals and other directives. Evaluators must realize that grading criteria contained herein cannot accommodate every situation. Written parameters must be tempered with mission objectives and, more importantly, mission/task accomplishment in the determination of overall aircrew performance. Requirements for each evaluation are as follows: **(T-3)**

2.2. Qualification Evaluations (T-3):

2.2.1. Written Examination Requisites: See Table 1.1

2.2.2. Emergency Procedures Evaluations: See paragraph 1.5.3.

2.2.3. Performance Phase: Areas 1 through 18 in Table 1.2 under CDA-OC and CDA-A will be evaluated, unless not applicable as noted.

2.3. Mission Certifications. Mission Certifications ensure individuals are capable of performing duties essential to the effective employment of the weapon system. Mission Certifications are accomplished IAW local training requirements and/or SQ/CC directions. Mission certification events are normally performed during Qualification evaluations, but may be performed on any mission/sortie with an instructor certified in that mission. **(T-3)**

2.4. General Crew Position Evaluation Criteria. The following general evaluation grading criteria are common to all crew positions, regardless of special mission qualification(s) and additional certifications, and will be used for all applicable evaluations:

2.4.1. AREA 1, Situational Awareness (C).

2.4.1.1. Q. Conducted the mission with a sense of understanding/comprehension and in a timely, efficient manner. Anticipated situations which would have adversely affected the mission and made appropriate decisions based on available information. Maintained overall good situational awareness. Recognized temporary loss of situational awareness in self or others and took appropriate action to regain awareness without detracting from mission accomplishment or jeopardizing safety. **(T-3)**

2.4.1.2. U. Decisions or lack thereof resulted in failure to accomplish the assigned mission. Demonstrated poor judgment or lost situational awareness to the extent that safety and/or mission accomplishment could have been compromised. **(T-3)**

2.4.2. AREA 2, Safety (C)

2.4.2.1. Q. Aware of and complied with all factors required for safe operations and mission accomplishment. **(T-3)**

2.4.2.2. U. Was not aware of safety factors or disregarded procedures to safely operate and conduct the mission. Conducted unsafe actions that jeopardized mission accomplishment and/or put crewmembers at risk of injury or death. Operated in a manner that could or did result in damage to the weapon system/equipment. **(T-3)**

2.4.3. AREA 3, Crew Discipline (C)

2.4.3.1. Q. Demonstrated strict professional crew discipline throughout all phases of the mission. Planned, briefed, executed, and debriefed mission in accordance with applicable instructions and directives. **(T-3)**

2.4.3.2. U. Failed to demonstrate strict professional crew discipline throughout all phases of the mission. Violated or failed to comply with applicable instructions and directives which could have jeopardized safety of crewmembers or mission accomplishment. **(T-3)**

2.4.4. AREA 4, Emergency Procedures/Equipment

2.4.4.1. Q. Recognized emergency situations or malfunctions and immediately demonstrated /explained appropriate response actions. Demonstrated/explained thorough knowledge of location and proper use of emergency equipment. Demonstrated/explained effective coordinated emergency actions with other crewmembers without delay or confusion. Followed appropriate checklists as required. Minor errors did not impact efficiencies in addressing the emergency. **(T-3)**

2.4.4.2. Q-. Recognized emergency situations or malfunctions but slow to demonstrate/explain appropriate response actions. Examinee demonstrated/explained correct procedures with minor errors and/or was slow to locate equipment and/or appropriate checklists. Slow or hesitant to demonstrate/explain coordinated emergency actions with other crewmembers. Minor checklist errors/omissions/deviations caused minor inefficiencies addressing the emergency situation/malfunction but did not exacerbate the situation. **(T-3)**

2.4.4.3. U. Failed to recognize emergency situations or malfunctions. Failed to demonstrate/explain proper response actions. Failed to demonstrate /explain knowledge of location or proper use of emergency equipment or checklists. Failed to demonstrate/explain coordinated emergency actions with other crewmembers. Checklist errors/omissions/deviations contributed to ineffective actions or exacerbating an emergency situation and/or malfunction. **(T-3)**

2.4.5. AREA 5, Mission Planning

2.4.5.1. Q. Led or contributed to mission planning efforts IAW procedures prescribed in applicable guidance manuals, instructions, and directives. Planning adequately addressed mission objectives and/or tasking. Planning adequately considered intelligence information, weapon system capability/operating status, and crew composition/ability with minor errors/deviations/omissions that did not impact mission effectiveness. **(T-3)**

2.4.5.2. Q-. Errors/deviations/omissions had minor impact on mission effectiveness or efficiencies, but did not impact mission accomplishment or jeopardize mission success. **(T-3)**

2.4.5.3. U. Failed to adequately lead mission planning effort. Failed to comply with procedures prescribed in applicable guidance manuals, instructions, and directives contributing to significant deficiencies in mission execution/accomplishment. Failed to lead or participate in all required briefings and/or planning meetings without appropriate approval. **(T-3)**

2.4.6. AREA 6, Briefing

2.4.6.1. Q. Led or contributed to briefing effort as appropriate. Well organized and presented in a logical sequence, appropriate timeframe, and professional manner. Effectively incorporated briefing/training aids and presented all training events and effective techniques required for accomplishing the mission. Briefing encompassed all required topics/areas of discussion IAW prescribed directives. Minor errors/omissions/deviations did not impact mission effectiveness or efficiencies. Crewmembers clearly understood roles, responsibilities, and mission requirements. Briefed Cybercrew Information File (CIF) Vol 1 Part B and crew Go/No-Go status. **(T-3)**

2.4.6.2. Q-. Led or contributed to briefing effort with minor errors/omissions/deviations. Some events out of sequence with some unnecessary redundancy. Briefing anomalies had minor impact on mission effectiveness but did not jeopardize mission success. **(T-3)**

2.4.6.3. U. Inadequate leadership or participation in briefing development and/or presentation. Disorganized and/or confusing presentation. Ineffective use of briefing/training aids. Failed to brief required topics/discussion areas prescribed in directives. Failed to present major training events. Failed to brief CIF Vol 1 Part B and crew Go/No-Go status. Errors/omissions/deviations impacted crew ability to accomplish the mission. Absent from briefing (whole or in-part) without appropriate supervisor approval. **(T-3)**

2.4.7. AREA 7, Pre-Mission Activity

2.4.7.1. Q. Initialized and signed-on the workstation. Reviewed all CIF Vol 1, Part B items and complied with Go/No-Go procedures prior to mission start. Demonstrated an understanding of systems and applications, supporting pre-mission activities. Accessed and verified all required mission materials for the crew position to include publications, checklists and working aids. Possessed all required personal and professional equipment in serviceable condition. Used applicable checklists as required. **(T-3)**

2.4.7.2. Q-. Deviations, omissions, or discrepancies did not jeopardize mission accomplishment, safety or security. Used applicable checklist; however omitted minor items that did not jeopardize mission accomplishment, safety or security. **(T-3)**

2.4.7.3. U. Failed to demonstrate an understanding of systems and applications. Pre-mission activities contained errors/omissions/deviations that could have or resulted in significant detraction from mission effectiveness. Failed to review CIF and/or comply with Go/No-Go procedures. Failed to determine/verify weapon system operational state and cybercrew readiness prior to on-watch period or entering tasked vulnerability period. **(T-3)**

2.4.8. AREA 8, Mission Checks/Checklist Procedures

2.4.8.1. Q. Performed all mission/operations checks as required. Efficient location and proficient/timely accomplishment of checklists. Adequately ensured, determined, and/or verified weapon system operational state and cybercrew readiness prior to on-station period or entering tasked vulnerability period. Ensured crew understanding of most up-to-date tasking(s) prior to on-watch or vulnerability period execution. Deviated from checklists and/or omitted steps only when appropriate and was able to substantiate justification. Minor errors/deviations/omissions did not detract from mission efficiencies nor jeopardize mission success. **(T-3)**

2.4.8.2. Q-. Same as qualified, except minor errors/deviations/omissions detracted from mission efficiencies but did not jeopardize overall mission success. **(T-3)**

2.4.8.3. U. Significant errors/deviations/omissions contributed to jeopardizing mission success and/or an emergency/unsafe condition. **(T-3)**

2.4.9. AREA 9, Crew Coordination

2.4.9.1. Q. Effectively coordinated with other crewmembers during all phases of the mission enabling efficient, well-coordinated actions. Demonstrated basic knowledge of other crewmembers' duties and responsibilities. Proactively provided direction and/or information to the crew; communicated in a clear and effective manner, actively sought other crewmember opinions and/or ideas, and asked for or provided constructive feedback as necessary. **(T-3)**

2.4.9.2. Q-. Minor breakdowns in communication did not detract from overall mission success. Limited in basic knowledge of other crewmembers' duties/responsibilities. Some prompting required from other crewmembers. **(T-3)**

2.4.9.3. U. Severe breakdowns in coordination led to mission ineffectiveness/failure or jeopardized safety of crewmembers. Lacked basic knowledge of other crewmember's duties and responsibilities. Unclear/lack of communication with other crewmembers put mission and/or safety of others at risk. **(T-3)**

2.4.10. AREA 10, Task Management

2.4.10.1. Q. Correctly identified, prioritized, and managed tasks based on existing and new information. Used available resources to manage workload and requested assistance when required. Effectively identified contingencies and solutions. **(T-3)**

2.4.10.2. Q-. Minor omissions or errors led to some inefficiencies but did not jeopardize mission accomplishment. Limited use of available resources to aid decision making, manage workload, and/or slow to request assistance from other crewmembers when needed. **(T-3)**

2.4.10.3. U. Inability or failure to identify contingencies. Ineffective decision making or errors/omissions placed mission accomplishment and/or safety of others at risk. Failed to identify, prioritize, or manage tasks leading to unsafe conditions or significant risk to mission accomplishment. **(T-3)**

2.4.11. AREA 11, Communication

2.4.11.1. Q. Timely and effective communication with external agencies and/or mission partners when required. Concise and accurate information passed using proper medium, terminology, format and/or brevity. Sound understanding and use of voice, email, chat, and collaborative tools to communicate mission essential information. Demonstrated a thorough understanding of COMSEC/OPSEC procedures. **(T-3)**

2.4.11.2. Q-. Minor errors/deviations/omissions in communications did not detract from overall mission accomplishment. **(T-3)**

2.4.11.3. U. Severe breakdowns in communication led to mission ineffectiveness/failure or jeopardized safety of others. Significant COMSEC/OPSEC errors or deviations jeopardized mission accomplishment. **(T-3)**

2.4.12. AREA 12, Systems Knowledge / Operations

2.4.12.1. Q. Demonstrated thorough knowledge of weapon system components (i.e. equipment, console, applications, tools, and/or software), performance characteristics, proper equipment use, and operating procedures. Correctly identified and applied proper action(s) for system malfunctions. Followed all applicable operating directives, guides, manuals, checklists etc. **(T-3)**

2.4.12.2. Q-. Minor errors/deviations/omissions did not detract from overall mission accomplishment. **(T-3)**

2.4.12.3. U. Demonstrated severe lack of knowledge in weapon system limitations, performance characteristics, equipment use or operating procedures. Failed to identify malfunctions and/or apply corrective actions. Failed to follow operating directives, guides and manuals resulting in equipment damage or mission failure. **(T-3)**

2.4.13. AREA 13, Reports and Transcripts

2.4.13.1. Q. Recognized all situations meeting reporting criteria. Provided timely, accurate, and correctly formatted reports and/or appropriate inputs to information management portals/collaborative databases. Complied with directives, tasking, policy and security procedures. **(T-3)**

2.4.13.2. Q-. Minor errors/deviations/omissions/latency on required reports and database inputs led to inefficiencies but did not affect mission accomplishment. **(T-3)**

2.4.13.3. U. Failed to recognize or report situations meeting applicable directives and/or criteria. Major errors/deviations/omissions/latency negatively impacted mission or data analysis. Failed to comply with policy and security procedures. **(T-3)**

2.4.14. AREA 14, Emergency/Criminal Information Reporting (C)

2.4.14.1. Q. Recognized/responded to alerts meeting potential unique reporting criteria. Distinguished between Significant Crime and Emergency Situation information and provided timely, accurate, and correctly formatted report and/or inputs for all notifications. Performed reporting procedures IAW AF policy and local directives. Used applicable checklists as required. **(T-3)**

2.4.14.2. U. Failed to recognize/respond to alerts meeting potential unique reporting criteria. Failed to execute reporting procedures IAW AF policy and local directives. Failed to use applicable checklist or omitted major checklist items that adversely affected mission accomplishment, safety or security. **(T-3)**

2.4.15. AREA 15, Classified Message Incident (C)

2.4.15.1. Q. Recognized/Responded to alerts meeting potential Classified Message Incident (CMI) criteria. Provided timely, accurate, and correctly formatted report and/or inputs for all notifications. Completed CMI steps to Identify, Notify and Isolate. Performed CMI procedures IAW AF policy and local directives. Used applicable checklists as required. **(T-3)**

2.4.15.2. U. Failed to recognize/respond to alerts meeting potential CMI criteria. Failed to execute CMI procedures IAW AF policy and local directives. Failed to use applicable checklists or omitted major checklist items that adversely affected mission accomplishment, safety or security. **(T-3)**

2.4.16. AREA 16, Post-Mission Activity

2.4.16.1. Q. Accomplished and/or supervised timely post-mission checks, system shutdown procedures, and workstation clean up IAW applicable checklists, guidance, and directives. **(T-3)**

2.4.16.2. Q-. Minor deviations, omissions, or errors led to inefficiencies but did not affect mission accomplishment. **(T-3)**

2.4.16.3. U. Deviations, omissions or errors in procedures jeopardized mission effectiveness, caused equipment damage, or endangered others. **(T-3)**

2.4.17. AREA 17, Debrief

2.4.17.1. Q. Thoroughly debriefed the mission and/or contributed to the debriefing by reconstructing operational events, comparing results with mission objectives, debriefing deviations, providing individual crew member feedback, and summarizing/documenting lessons learned. Organized IAW guidance/directives and professionally presented in a logical sequence using available briefing aids. Used applicable checklist(s) as required. **(T-3)**

2.4.17.2. Q-. Led or contributed to debriefing effort with minor errors/omissions/deviations. **(T-3)**

2.4.17.3. U. Inadequate leadership or participation in debriefing development and/or presentation. Disorganized and/or confusing presentation. Ineffective use of briefing/training aids. Failed to reconstruct operational events, compare results with mission objectives, debrief deviations, provide corrective crew guidance as appropriate and/or address lessons learned. Absent from debriefing (whole or in-part) without appropriate supervisor approval. **(T-3)**

2.5. Operations Controller Specific Evaluation Criteria. The following evaluation grading criteria is common to the Operations Controller crew position and will be used for all applicable evaluations:

2.5.1. AREA 18, Mission Management.

2.5.1.1. Q. Accurately identified, effectively prioritized, and efficiently managed the mission based on tasking/Rules of Engagement (ROE), planned information, and tactical situation. Identified contingencies, gathered data, and clearly communicated task priorities/decisions to crewmembers in coordination with outside agencies. Used available resources to manage workload, monitor crew activity, and aid in decision making. As necessary, effectively planned and integrated with Composite Force (CF) or Mutual Support (MS) agencies to enhance mission effectiveness and achieve objectives. **(T-3)**

2.5.1.2. Q-. Minor omissions and/or errors did not affect safety of crewmembers or effective mission accomplishment. **(T-3)**

2.5.1.3. U. Failed to identify, prioritize, or manage mission tasks leading to possible unsafe conditions or significant risk to mission accomplishment. Failed to identify contingencies, gather data, and clearly communicate task priorities/decisions to crewmembers and outside agencies. Inadequate or incorrect planning/integration of CF or MS agencies resulted in mission failure. **(T-3)**

2.6. Web Risk Assessment (WRA) SMQ Specific Evaluation Criteria. The following evaluation grading criteria is for the WRA special mission qualification and will be used for all applicable evaluations:

2.6.1. AREA 19, WRA Collection and Analysis (M)

2.6.1.1. Q. Demonstrated thorough knowledge of WRA system components (i.e. equipment, console, applications, tools, and/or software), performance characteristics, proper equipment use, and operating procedures. Correctly identified and applied proper action(s) for system malfunctions. Followed all applicable operating directives, guides, manuals, checklists etc. **(T-3)**

2.6.1.2. Q-. Minor errors, omissions, or delays detracted from mission efficiency but did not jeopardize overall mission accomplishment. **(T-3)**

2.6.1.3. U. Demonstrated severe lack of knowledge in WRA system limitations, performance characteristics, equipment use or operating procedures. Failed to identify malfunctions and/or apply corrective actions. Failed to follow operating directives, guides and manuals resulting in equipment damage or mission failure. **(T-3)**

2.7. D V M S (DVMS) SMQ Specific Evaluation Criteria. The following evaluation grading criteria is for the WRA special mission qualification and will be used for all applicable evaluations:

2.7.1. AREA 20, DVMS Collection and Analysis (M)

2.7.1.1. Q. Demonstrated thorough knowledge of DVMS system components (i.e. equipment, console, applications, tools, and/or software), performance characteristics, proper equipment use, and operating procedures. Correctly identified and applied proper action(s) for system malfunctions. Followed all applicable operating directives, guides, manuals, checklists etc. **(T-3)**

2.7.1.2. Q-. Minor errors, omissions, or delays detracted from mission efficiency but did not jeopardize overall mission accomplishment. **(T-3)**

2.7.1.3. U. Demonstrated severe lack of knowledge in DVMS system limitations, performance characteristics, equipment use or operating procedures. Failed to identify malfunctions and/or apply corrective actions. Failed to follow operating directives, guides and manuals resulting in equipment damage or mission failure. **(T-3)**

2.8. SCOUT SMQ Specific Evaluation Criteria. The following evaluation grading criteria is for the SCOUT special mission qualification and will be used for all applicable evaluations:

2.8.1. AREA 21, SCOUT Collection and Analysis (M)

2.8.1.1. Q. Demonstrated thorough knowledge of FIDELIS SCOUT system components (i.e. equipment, console, applications, tools, and/or software), performance characteristics, proper equipment use, and operating procedures. Correctly identified and applied proper action(s) for system malfunctions. Followed all applicable operating directives, guides, manuals, checklists etc. **(T-3)**

2.8.1.2. Q-. Minor errors, omissions, or delays detracted from mission efficiency but did not jeopardize overall mission accomplishment. **(T-3)**

2.8.1.3. U. Demonstrated severe lack of knowledge in FIDELIS SCOUT system limitations, performance characteristics, equipment use or operating procedures. Failed to identify malfunctions and/or apply corrective actions. Failed to follow operating directives, guides and manuals resulting in equipment damage or mission failure. **(T-3)**

2.9. Radio Frequency (RF) SMQ Specific Evaluation Criteria. The following evaluation grading criteria is for the WRA special mission qualification and will be used for all applicable evaluations:

2.9.1. AREA 22, RF Collection and Analysis (M)

2.9.1.1. Q. Demonstrated thorough knowledge of RF system components (i.e. equipment, console, applications, tools, and/or software), performance characteristics, proper equipment use, and operating procedures. Correctly identified and applied proper action(s) for system malfunctions. Followed all applicable operating directives, guides, manuals, checklists etc. **(T-3)**

2.9.1.2. Q-. Minor errors, omissions, or delays detracted from mission efficiency but did not jeopardize overall mission accomplishment. **(T-3)**

2.9.1.3. U. Demonstrated severe lack of knowledge in RF system limitations, performance characteristics, equipment use or operating procedures. Failed to identify malfunctions and/or apply corrective actions. Failed to follow operating directives, guides and manuals resulting in equipment damage or mission failure. **(T-3)**

Chapter 3

INSTRUCTOR EVALUATIONS AND GRADING CRITERIA

3.1. General. Grading criteria contained herein cannot accommodate every situation. Written parameters must be tempered with sortie objectives, evaluator judgment, and task accomplishment in the determination of overall aircrew performance. **(T-2).**

3.2. Instructor Upgrade and Qualification Requisites. Prior to an initial instructor evaluation, instructor examinees must have completed all requisites for instructor upgrade consideration, nomination and training IAW AFI 17-202V1, AFI 17-2CDAV1, and all applicable supplemental guidance. **(T-2).**

3.3. Instructor Qualification Evaluations: When possible, units should strive to combine instructor evaluations (initial and recurring/periodic) with periodic QUAL evaluations. Instructor evaluations can only be combined with QUAL evaluations when the examinee is in their periodic QUAL eligibility period. There is no eligibility period associated with an instructor qualification; however, instructor qualifications will expire after the 17th month from the previous instructor qualification evaluation. See paragraph 3.5 for documentation guidance. **(T-2)**

3.3.1. Initial instructor evaluations should be conducted with a student occupying the applicable cybercrew position whenever possible. Recurring or periodic Instructor Evaluations may be conducted with the SEE role playing as the student.

3.3.2. The instructor examinee will monitor all phases of the mission from an advantageous position and be prepared to demonstrate or explain any area or procedure. The SEE will particularly note the instructor's ability to recognize student difficulties and provide effective, timely instruction and/or corrective action. The SEE should also evaluate the grade assigned and the completed grade sheet or event training form for the student on all initial instructor checks. **(T-2).**

3.3.3. The student will perform those duties prescribed by the instructor for the mission/sortie being accomplished. If an actual student is not available, the SEE will identify to the examinee (prior to the mission) the level of performance to be expected from the SEE acting as the student. If this option is utilized, at least one event or briefing must be instructed. **(T-2).**

3.3.4. Periodic instructor evaluations will be administered in conjunction with required periodic qualification evaluations. The examinee must occupy the primary duty position for an adequate period of time to demonstrate proficiency in the crew position with required qualification evaluations. All instructor evaluations will include a pre-mission and post-mission briefing. **(T-2)**

3.3.5. Awarding a "U" in any of the instructor evaluation criteria areas will result in a Q3 for the overall instructor grade. The overall grade for the instructor portion of the evaluation will be no higher than the lowest overall grade awarded under QUAL. **(T-2)**

3.4. Instructor Evaluation Grading Criteria. All instructor evaluation criteria must be observed and graded to ensure a complete evaluation. Specific requirements for each evaluation are as follows:

3.4.1. AREA 19, Instructional Ability

3.4.1.1. Q. Demonstrated ability to communicate effectively. Provided appropriate corrective guidance when necessary. Planned ahead and made timely decisions. Correctly analyzed student errors. **(T-2)**

3.4.1.2. Q-. Minor discrepancies in the above criteria that did not adversely impact student progress. **(T-2)**

3.4.1.3. U. Unable to effectively communicate with the student. Did not provide corrective action where necessary. Did not plan ahead or anticipate student problems. Incorrectly analyzed student errors. Adversely impacted student progress. **(T-2)**

3.4.2. AREA 21, Instructional Briefings/Critique

3.4.2.1. Q. Briefings were well organized, accurate, and thorough. Reviewed student's present level of training and defined mission events to be performed. Demonstrated ability during critique to reconstruct the mission/sortie, offer mission analysis, and provide corrective guidance where appropriate. Completed all training documents according to prescribed directives. Appropriate grades awarded. **(T-2)**

3.4.2.2. Q-. As above but with minor errors or omissions in briefings, critique, or training documents that did not adversely impact student progress. **(T-2)**

3.4.2.3. U. Pre-mission or post-mission briefings were marginal or nonexistent. Did not review student's training folder or past performance. Failed to adequately critique student or conducted an incomplete mission analysis which compromised learning. Student strengths or weaknesses were not identified. Adversely impacted student progress. Inappropriate grades awarded. Overlooked or omitted major discrepancies. **(T-2)**

3.4.3. AREA 22, Demonstration and Performance

3.4.3.1. Q. Effectively demonstrated procedures and techniques. Demonstrated thorough knowledge of weapon system/components, procedures, and all applicable publications and regulations. **(T-2)**

3.4.3.2. Q-. Minor discrepancies in the above criteria that did not adversely impact student progress. **(T-2)**

3.4.3.3. U. Did not demonstrate correct procedure or technique. Insufficient depth of knowledge about weapon system/components, procedures, or proper source material. Adversely impacted student progress. **(T-2)**

3.5. Instructor Evaluation Documentation.

3.5.1. Instructor Qualification Evaluations will be documented as a SPOT evaluation on the AF Form 4418 and AF Form 4420 and maintained in the member's cyber crew qualification folder IAW AFI 17-202V2, applicable higher headquarters supplements, and local supplemental guidance. (T-2) Additional Instructor Evaluation documentation is as follows:

3.5.2. Initial Instructor Qualification Evaluation. Initial instructor evaluations will not be combined with any other evaluations. **(T-2)**

3.5.2.1. Upon completion of the AF Form 4418, place the appropriate corresponding entry onto the AF Form 4420, *Individual's Record of Duties and Qualifications*. **(T-2)**

3.5.3. Recurring/Periodic Instructor Qualification Evaluation.

3.5.3.1. If conducted in conjunction with the Instructor Examinee's periodic QUAL evaluation, the Instructor Qualification Evaluation will be documented on the same AF Form 4418, placing SPOT in the second "Evaluation Type below the QUAL annotation. Place a statement in comments section that the evaluation was a periodic QUAL evaluation in conjunction with periodic or recurring Instructor Qualification Evaluation. Place any comments specific to the Instructor portion of the evaluation separately from the QUAL portion of the evaluation. **(T-3)**

3.5.3.2. If the Instructor Qualification Evaluation is not in conjunction with a periodic QUAL evaluation, document the evaluation as a SPOT in the first "Evaluation Type" block and place a statement in the comments section that the evaluation was recurring or periodic Instructor Qualification Evaluation. **(T-2)**

3.5.3.3. Upon completion of the AF Form 4418, place the appropriate corresponding entry onto the AF Form 4420. **(T-2)**

3.5.4. Letter of Certification (Letter of Xs).

3.5.4.1. Upon the successful completion of an Instructor Qualification Evaluation, units will ensure the crewmembers instructor status is reflected on the Letter of Xs **(T-2)**

3.5.4.2. Upon the expiration of a qualification or failure of an Instructor Qualification Evaluation, units will ensure the crewmembers instructor status is reflected on the Letter of Xs. **(T-2)**

Chapter 4

SEE OBJECTIVITY EVALUATIONS AND GRADING CRITERIA

4.1. General. SEE Objectivity Evaluations are a vehicle for commanders to upgrade crewmembers for SEE qualification and a tool to monitor the evaluator crew force's adherence to Stan/Eval directives. Grading criteria cannot accommodate every situation. Written parameters must be tempered with sortie objectives, evaluator judgment, and task accomplishment in the determination of overall examinee performance. The criteria contained in this chapter are established by experience, policies, and procedures in weapon system manuals and other directives. The criteria contained in this chapter are applicable to all SEE Objectivity Evaluations for CDA crewmembers. **(T-2)**

4.2. Evaluator Upgrade and Qualification Requisites. Evaluator upgrade candidates will be selected from the most qualified and competent instructors. **(T-2)**

4.2.1. Wing/Group/Squadron. SEE Upgrade candidate nominations will be approved by the OG/CC in writing. Once approved, candidates must complete all SEE training IAW AFI 17-202V2, this instruction, and all applicable supplemental guidance. As a minimum, SEE training will consist of:

4.2.1.1. Local SEE academics/instruction covering all Stan/Eval programs and procedures. Training completion should be documented on a locally developed OG/CC checklist along with a signed certificate from the OG/CC or OG/CD. Both checklist and certificate will be kept on file by the unit Stan/Eval office. **(T-2)**

4.2.1.2. The candidate observing one entire evaluation performed by a qualified SEE. NOTE: To the maximum extent possible, SEE Upgrade candidates should observe evaluations conducted within the weapon system for which they are qualified, however when not practical, the observed evaluation may be conducted with a qualified SEE in the same Group regardless of weapon system or crew position. Training completion should be documented on a locally developed OG/CC checklist and maintained in the unit Stan/Eval office. **(T-2)**

4.2.1.3. Completion of a SEE Objectivity Evaluation under the supervision of a qualified examiner. NOTE: The SEE Objectivity will be conducted within the weapon system and crew position for which the SEE Upgrade candidate (SEE Examinee) maintains qualification. See paragraph 4.5 for SEE Objectivity Evaluation (AF Form 4418) documentation guidance. **(T-2)**

4.2.2. MAJCOM/NAF. MAJCOM and NAF CDA evaluators will be qualified in the CDA weapon system and maintain at a minimum BMC currency/proficiency status IAW AFI 17-2 *Cyberspace Defense Analysis (CDA) Training, Volume* 1 (AFI17-2CDAV1) and all applicable supplemental guidance. Additionally, MAJCOM and NAF evaluators for the CDA weapon system will have previous SEE experience at the wing, group, or squadron level in either in the CDA WS or another WS/mission. **(T-2)**

4.3. SEE Objectivity Evaluations. There is no eligibility period or expiration date associated with a SEE Objectivity Evaluation. Once obtained, crewmembers maintain SEE qualification unless they fail a QUAL evaluation, fail an Instructor evaluation, fail a SEE Objectivity Evaluation, their weapon system QUAL expires, or upon their SEE appointment being revoked/rescinded by the appointing official. See paragraph 4.5. for SEE Objectivity Evaluation documentation guidance. **(T-2)**

4.3.1. Only a qualified cyberspace weapon system SEE may administer a SEE Objectivity Evaluation to a cyberspace SEE examinee. SEE Objectivity Evaluations may be administered by SEE Examiners qualified in a different cyberspace weapon system type or crew position from the SEE examinee. NOTE: This is common when the SEE Objectivity Evaluation is in conjunction with a higher headquarters inspection. **(T-2)**

4.3.2. SEE Objectivity Evaluations will not be combined with any other type evaluation. **(T-2)**

4.3.3. SEE Objectivity Evaluations will ensure the SEE examinee (for example in the case of a SEE Objectivity conducted as part of a higher headquarters inspection) observes and grades the entire mission activity of the QUAL examinee. Mission activity is defined as all mission planning, briefing, execution, and debrief activities for the mission/sortie. **(T-2)**

4.3.4. The SEE Upgrade candidate or SEE Examinee will brief the qualified SEE Examiner on all observations, grades, commendable/discrepancies (if any), recommended additional training, and other mission related debrief topics prior to debriefing the QUAL examinee and/or examinee's supervisor. **(T-2)**

4.3.5. The SEE Upgrade candidate or SEE Examinee will complete the AF Form 4418 and have the SEE Examiner review it for completeness and accuracy. The SEE Examiner's signature block and signature (not signature/block of the SEE Upgrade candidate or SEE Examinee) will be entered on the AF Form 4418. **(T-2)**

4.3.6. The SEE Examiner will administer a pre-brief and debrief to the SEE Examinee. **(T-2)**

4.3.7. For SEE Upgrade candidates, SEE Objectivity evaluations will only be administered for observed INIT QUAL or periodic QUAL evaluations. Additionally, the QUAL evaluation may not be combined with an Instructor Evaluation. **(T-2)**

4.4. SEE Objectivity Evaluation Grading Criteria. All SEE Objectivity Evaluation Criteria must be observed and graded to ensure a complete evaluation. The following grading criteria will be used by SEEs when conducting SEE Objectivity Evaluations. A grade of Q- requiring additional training or a grade of U in any area for the SEE Objectivity Examinee will require an overall rating of "3". Cumulative deviations will be considered when determining the overall rating of either "1" or "3". Specific requirements for each evaluation are as follows:

4.4.1. AREA 23, Directives Compliance/Understanding

4.4.1.1. Q. Complied with and understood all operational directives and guidance. Complied with all directives pertaining to the administration of a positional and/or instructor evaluation. **(T-2)**

4.4.1.2. Q-. Complied with and understood most directives. Deviations did not jeopardize the mission, the effectiveness of the evaluation, or crew safety. **(T-2)**

4.4.1.3. U. Failed to comply and/or understand directives jeopardizing mission effectiveness, effectiveness of the evaluation, and/or crew safety. **(T-2)**

4.4.2. AREA 25, Stan/Eval Examiner (SEE) Briefing

4.4.2.1. Q. Thoroughly briefed the examinee on the conduct of the evaluation, mission requirements, responsibilities, grading criteria, and examiner actions/position during the evaluation. **(T-2)**

4.4.2.2. Q-. Items were omitted during the briefing causing minor confusion. Did not fully brief the examinee as to the conduct and purpose of the evaluation. **(T-2)**

4.4.2.3. U. Examiner failed to adequately brief the examinee. **(T-2)**

4.4.3. AREA 26, Performance Assessment and Grading **(T-2)**

4.4.3.1. Q. Identified all discrepancies and assigned proper area grade. Awarded the appropriate overall grade based on the examinee's performance. **(T-2)**

4.4.3.2. Q-. Most discrepancies were identified. Failed to assign Q- grade when appropriate. Assigned performance discrepancies within standards. Awarded an overall grade without consideration of cumulative deviations in the examinee's performance. **(T-2)**

4.4.3.3. U. Failed to identify most discrepancies. Did not award a grade commensurate with overall performance. Failed to assign additional training when warranted. **(T-2)**

4.4.4. AREA 27, Additional Training Recommendation

4.4.4.1. Q. Recommended proper additional training when warranted. NOTE: If the QUAL Examinee's performance (i.e. Q1) does not warrant the recommendation of additional training, the SEE Examinee will verbally explain to the SEE Examiner the proper procedures for recommending additional training. This may be accomplished as part of the SEE Objectivity pre-brief or debrief. **(T-2)**

4.4.4.2. Q-. Additional training recommended was insufficient to ensure the examinee would achieve proper level of qualification. SEE Examinee's discrepancy or omission was correctable prior to QUAL Examinee debrief and in the SEE Objectivity debrief. **(T-2)**

4.4.4.3. U. Failed to assign additional training when warranted. **(T-2)**

4.4.5. AREA 28, Examinee Critique / Debrief

4.4.5.1. Q. Thoroughly debriefed the examinee on all aspects of the evaluation. Reconstructed and debriefed all key mission events, providing instruction and references to directives and guidance when applicable. **(T-2)**

4.4.5.2. Q-. Some errors/omissions in reconstructing key mission events, in discussing deviations/discrepancies, referencing directives/guidance and debriefing assigned grades. Did not advise the examinee of all additional training when warranted. Errors/omissions did not adversely affect overall evaluation effectiveness. **(T-2)**

4.4.5.3. U. Failed to discuss any assigned area grades or the overall rating. Changed grades without briefing the examinee and/or supervisor. Did not debrief key mission events and/or provide appropriate instruction during critique. **(T-2)**

4.4.6. AREA 29, Supervisor Debrief

4.4.6.1. Q. Thoroughly debriefed the QUAL examinee's supervisor. Reconstructed and debriefed all key mission events pertinent to the QUAL examinee's performance, citing references to directives and guidance when applicable. Briefed the supervisor on all discrepancies requiring additional training, downgraded areas, and the overall qualification rating being assigned to the QUAL examinee. NOTE: If the QUAL examinee's performance (i.e. Q1) does not warrant a supervisor debrief, the SEE examinee will verbally explain to the SEE examiner the proper procedures for conducting a supervisor debriefing. This may be accomplished as part of the SEE Objectivity pre-brief or debrief. **(T-2)**

4.4.6.2. Q-. Some errors/omissions in reconstructing key mission events, discussing deviations/discrepancies, referencing directives/guidance, debriefing of assigned additional training, and assigning of QUAL examinee grades/ratings with the supervisor. Errors/omissions did not adversely affect overall evaluation effectiveness. **(T-2)**

4.4.6.3. U. Failed to discuss any observed discrepancies, assigned area downgrades or the overall rating with the supervisor. Changed grades without briefing the examinee and/or supervisor. Did not debrief key mission events contributing to the QUAL examinees overall performance and assigned qualification rating. **(T-2)**

4.4.7. AREA 30, SEE Performance and Evaluation Documentation

4.4.7.1. Q. SEE examinee performed as briefed and ensured a thorough evaluation of the QUAL and/or instructor evaluation examinee. SEE examinee correctly documented the QUAL or SPOT (i.e. for instructor check rides) examinee's performance on the AF Form 4418. **(T-2)**

4.4.7.2. Q-. Minor errors or discrepancies during the mission did not impact or detract from the QUAL or SPOT examinees' performance. Minor errors/discrepancies in accomplishing documentation. **(T-2)**

4.4.7.3. U. Major errors/disruptions impacted or detracted from the QUAL or SPOT examinee's performance and/or prevented a thorough evaluation. Failure or major errors/discrepancies in accomplishing documentation. **(T-2)**

4.5. SEE Objectivity Evaluation Documentation. SEE Objectivity Evaluations will be documented as a SPOT evaluation on the AF Form 4418 and AF Form 4420 and maintained in the member's cyber crew qualification folder IAW AFI 17-202V2 and applicable higher headquarters/local supplemental guidance. **(T-2)**

4.5.1. Letter of Certification (Letter of Xs).

4.5.1.1. Upon the successful completion of a SEE Objectivity Evaluation, units will ensure the crewmember's SEE status is reflected on the Letter of Xs. **(T-2)**

4.5.1.2. Upon the decertification or loss of SEE qualification, units will ensure the Letter of Xs appropriately reflects the crewmember's status. **(T-2)**

WILLIAM J. BENDER, Lt Gen, USAF
Chief of Information Dominance and Chief
Information Officer

Attachment 1

GLOSSARY OF REFERENCES AND SUPPORTING INFORMATION

References

Privacy Act of 1974 *(5 U.S.C. 552a)*

AFPD 17-2, *Cyberspace Operations*, 12 April 2016

AFI 17-2 *Cyberspace Defense Analysis (CDA) Training, Volume* 1

AFI 17-202 Volume 1, *Cybercrew Training*, 2 Apr 2014, *Incorporating Change* 1, 6 May 2015

AFI 17-202 Volume 2, *Cybercrew Standardization and Evaluation Program*, 15 October 2014, *Incorporating Change 1,* 2 July 2015

AFI 17-202 Volume 3, *Cyberspace Operations and Procedures*, 15 February 2014

AFI 33-360, *Publications and Forms Management*, 1 December 2015

AFMAN 33-363, *Management of Records*, 1 March 2008

Adopted Forms

AF Form 679, *Air Force Publication Compliance Item Waiver Request/Approval*

AF Form 847, *Recommendation for Change of Publication*

AF Form 4418, *Certificate of Cybercrew Qualification*

AF Form 4420, *Individual's Record of Duties and Qualifications*

Abbreviations and Acronyms

AF—Air Force

AFI—Air Force Instruction

AFIN—Air Force Information Network

AFMAN—Air Force Manual

AFPD—Air Force Policy Document

AFRC—Air Force Reserve Command

AFSPC—Air Force Space Command

ANG—Air National Guard

CC—Commander

CDA—Cyber Defense Analysis

CDA/A—Cyber Defense Analysis Analyst

CDA/OC—Cyber Defense Analysis Operations Controller

CF—Composite Force

CIF—Crew Information File

CMI—Classified Message Incident

CRM—Crew Resource Management

CTD—Cybercrew Training Device

EPE—Emergency Procedure Evaluation

HQ—Headquarters

IAW—In Accordance With

INSTR—Instructor

LEP—List of Effective Pages

MAJCOM—Major Command

MS—Mutual Support

MSN—Mission Qualification

NAF—Numbered Air Force

N/N—No-notice

OC—Operations Controller

OG—Operations Group

OG/CC—Operations Group Commander

OGV—Operations Group Standardization/Evaluation

OPR—Office of Primary Responsibility

QUAL—Qualification

ROE—Rules of Engagement

SEE—Stan/Eval Examiner

SPOT—Spot Evaluation

SMQ—Special Mission Qualification

SQ—Squadron

STAN/EVAL—Standardization and Evaluation

WRA—Web Risk Assessment

WG—Wing

Terms

Commendable—An observed exemplary demonstration of knowledge and/or or noteworthy ability to perform by the examinee in a particular graded area/subarea, tactic, technique, procedure, and/or task.

Cyberspace Operations Controller (CDA/OC)—Cyberspace operator qualified to perform operations controller duties.

Cyberspace Operations Analyst (CDA/A)—Cyberspace operator qualified to perform operations analyst duties.

Deficiency—Demonstrated level of knowledge or ability to perform is inadequate, insufficient, or short of meeting required or expected proficiency.

Deviation—Performing an action not in sequence with current procedures, directives, or regulations. Performing action(s) out of sequence due to unusual or extenuating circumstances is not considered a deviation. In some cases, momentary deviations may be acceptable; however, cumulative deviations will be considered in determining the overall qualification level.

Discrepancy—Any observed deviations/errors/omissions, individually or cumulative, that detracts from the examinee's performance in obtaining a Q for a specific grading area/subarea.

Error—Departure from standard procedure. Performing incorrect actions or recording

inaccurate information.

Stan/Eval Examiner (SEE)—A crew member designated to administer evaluations.

Inadequate—Lack or underutilization of available crew aids or resources to effectively/efficiently make operational and tactical decisions, gain/maintain situational awareness, or accomplish a task.

Inappropriate—Excessive reliance on crew aids/other resources or utilizing a crew aid/ resource outside its intended use.

Instructor—Crew member trained, qualified, and certified by the squadron commander as an instructor to perform both ground and in-flight training.

Instructor Supervision—When a current instructor, supervises a maneuver or training event.

Major (deviation/error/omission)—Detracted from task accomplishment, adversely affected use of equipment, or violated safety.

Minor (deviation/error/omission)—Did not detract from task accomplishment, adversely affect use of equipment, or violate safety.

Omission—To leave out a required action or annotation.

Supervised Training Status—Crew member will perform weapon system duties under instructor supervision as designated by the squadron commander or evaluator.

Cyberspace Training Devices—All trainers, computer assisted instruction, sound-on-slide programs, videos, and mockups designed to prepare students for operations training or augment prescribed continuation training.

BY ORDER OF THE SECRETARY
OF THE AIR FORCE

AIR FORCE INSTRUCTION 17-2CDA
VOLUME 3

9 JUNE 2017

Cyberspace

**AIR FORCE CYBERSPACE DEFENSE
ANALYSIS (CDA) OPERATIONS AND
PROCEDURES**

COMPLIANCE WITH THIS PUBLICATION IS MANDATORY

ACCESSIBILITY: Publications and forms are available downloading or ordering on the e-Publishing website at **www.e-Publishing.af.mil**

RELEASABILITY: There are no releasability restrictions on this publication

OPR: AF/A3CX/A6CX

Certified by: AF/A3C/A6C
(Col Charles Cornelius)
Pages: 17

This volume implements Air Force (AF) Policy Directive (AFPD) 17-2, *Cyberspace Operations* and references AFI 17-202 Volume 3, *Cyberspace Operations and Procedures*. It applies to all Cyberspace Defense Analysis (CDA) units. This publication applies to all military and civilian AF personnel, members of the AF Reserve Command (AFRC), Air National Guard (ANG), and contractor support personnel in accordance with appropriate provisions contained in memoranda support agreements and AF contracts. This publication requires the collection and or maintenance of information protected by the *Privacy Act (PA) of 1947*. The authorities to collect and maintain the records prescribed in this publication are *Title 10 United States Code*, Chapter 857 and *Executive Order* 9397, *Numbering System for Federal Accounts Relating to Individual Persons*, 30 November 1943, as amended by *Executive Order* 13478, Amendments to Executive Order 9397 Relating to Federal Agency Use of Social Security Numbers, November 18, 2008.

The authorities to waive wing/unit level requirements in this publication are identified with a Tier ("T-0, T-1, T-2, T-3") number following the compliance statement. See AFI 33-360, *Publications and Forms Management*, Table 1.1 for a description of the authorities associated with the Tier numbers. Submit requests for waivers through the chain of command to the appropriate Tier waiver approval authority, or alternately, to the publication OPR for non-tiered compliance items. Refer recommended changes and questions about this publication to the Office of Primary Responsibility (OPR) using AF Form 847, *Recommendation for Change of Publication*; route AF Forms 847 from the field through Major Command (MAJCOM) publications/forms managers to AF/A3C/A6C. Ensure all records created as a result of processes prescribed in this publication are maintained in accordance with AF Manual (AFMAN) 33-363, *Management of Records* and disposed of in accordance with (IAW) the AF Records Disposition Schedule (RDS).

Chapter 1

GENERAL GUIDANCE

1.1. References, Abbreviations, Acronyms, and Terms. See Attachment 1.

1.2. General. This volume, in conjunction with other governing directives, prescribes procedures for operating the CDA weapon system under most circumstance, but it is not a substitute for sound judgment or common sense. It directs actions, assigns responsibilities and prescribes procedures for generating and employing AF CDA mission crews. Procedures not specifically addressed may be accomplished if they enhance safe and effective mission accomplishment.

1.3. Waivers. Unless another approval authority is cited ("T-0, T-1, T-2, T-3"), waiver authority for this volume is the MAJCOM/A3 (or equivalent). Submit requests for waivers using AF Form 679, *Air Force Publication Compliance Item Waiver Request/Approval* through the chain of command to the appropriate Tier waiver approval authority. If approved, waivers remain in effect for the life of the published guidance, unless the waiver authority specifies a shorter period of time, cancels in writing, or issues a change that alters the basis for the waiver.

1.4. Deviations. In the case of an urgent requirement or emergency the Cyberspace Mission Supervisor (CMS) will take appropriate action(s) to ensure safe operations.

1.5. Processing Changes.

1.5.1. The submitting MAJCOM will forward information copies of AF Forms 847 to all other MAJCOMS that use this publication. Using MAJCOMs will forward comments on AF Forms 847 to the OPR.

1.5.2. OPR will:

1.5.2.1. Coordinate all changes to the basic instruction with affected MAJCOM/A3s. **(T-2)**

1.5.2.2. Forward change recommendations to MAJCOM/A3 for staffing and AF/A3 approval. **(T-2)**

1.6. Supplements. Guidance for supplementing this publication is in AFI 33-360. Supplements will not duplicate, alter, amend or be less restrictive than the provisions of this instruction. **(T-2)**

Chapter 2

CREW DUTIES, POSITIONS, AND PROCEDURES

2.1. Crew Stations. Crewmembers shall be in their seats on the operations floor during the mission execution. Crewmembers will notify their CDA Operations Controller (CDA-OC) prior to departing their assigned crew duty station. **(T-3)**

2.2. Crew Duties. Crewmembers are responsible for successful sortie completion. Crews are responsible for the safe, effective use of the weapon system. A crew brief will be accomplished before each mission execution to ensure an understanding of all mission aspects. **(T-3)**

2.3. Crew Positions.

2.3.1. Cyberspace Defense Analysis/Operations Controller (CDA-OC). Directs, manages, and provides oversight for sorties and cybercrew personnel, as well as enforcing policies and procedures to ensure successful mission accomplishment. Performs quality control on all reports and mission logging and is also the Crew Lead during a sortie. In addition to CDA-A duties, the CDA-OC duties include:

2.3.1.1. Managing crew resources and safe mission accomplishment. **(T-3)**

2.3.1.2. Welfare of the crew. **(T-3)**

2.3.1.3. Ensuring risk management decision matrices are performed prior to mission briefing. **(T-3)**

2.3.1.4. Leads crew mission planning, mission brief, and debrief. **(T-3)**

2.3.1.5. Responsible for any post mission reporting. **(T-3)**

2.3.2. Cyberspace Defense Analysis/Analyst (CDA-A). Operates the CDA weapon system, conducting enduring enterprise-wide monitoring, analysis, and reporting to minimize the type and amount of unclassified information supporting global AF Operations (air, space, and cyberspace) available for exploitation. CDA-A duties include:

2.3.2.1. Perform and sign Operational Risk Management (ORM) as part of Sign Go/No-Go. **(T-3)**

2.3.2.2. Read the Crew Information File (CFI). **(T-3)**

2.3.2.3. Review the AFCYBER Cyberspace Tasking Order (CTO) and Special Instructions (SPINS) for updates. **(T-3)**

2.3.2.4. Process and analyze assigned data alerts from CDA/OC. **(T-3)**

2.3.2.5. Notify CDA/OC with flagged alerts. **(T-3)**

2.3.2.6. Identify and report system errors to the CDA/OC. **(T-3)**

2.3.2.7. Make recommendations to modify, add, change or delete keywords and signatures. **(T-3)**

2.3.3. The Web Risk Assessment (WRA) operator is a special mission qualification and provides the capability for continuous and systematic analysis of content and information resident on AF owned, leased, or operated web sites. Minimizing the vulnerability of AF information posted on an AF public and private unclassified Web sites by identifying sensitive information and personal data to the information owner and web management community for review/action. Conduct cross sectional analyses of AF web content, trend analyses, and data aggregation where unclassified information from multiple Web sites could pose an unacceptable risk to ongoing military operations and personnel.

2.3.4. The Deployed Voice Monitoring System (DVMS) operator is a special mission qualification and provides a mobile capability to monitor and analyze digital telephone traffic at locations not directly connected to a major cyberspace hub and Voice Protection System through the use of portable devices connected appliances/cache devices installed at AF installations. Data collected can be either analyzed locally or exported to the local CDA unit for offsite analysis.

2.3.5. The FIDELIS SCOUT (SCOUT) operator is a special mission qualification and provides a mobile capability to monitor e-mail and Internet based Capabilities (IbC) for use at locations that do not fall under the AF Gateway architecture. The system consists of a Fidelis XPS Sensor, a Fidelis XPS Command Post, and the Fidelis XPS interface all in one laptop.

2.3.6. The Radio Frequency (RF) operator is a special mission qualifications and provides the capability to monitor and collect RF communications to include most cellular transmissions (not capable of "breaking" commonly used encryption schemes), pager transmissions, Ultra High Frequency (UHF), and Very High Frequency (VHF) communications. Data collected can be either analyzed locally or exported to a CDA unit for offsite analysis.

2.4. Crew Manning. See table 2.1 for standard crew compliment requirements. **(T-3)**

Table 2.1. Standard Crew Manning.

Weapon System	CDA-OC	CDA-A	Total Crew
CDA	1	3	4

2.5. Inexperienced crewmembers will not perform operations, until certified. **(T-1)**

2.6. Crew Qualification. Each person assigned as a primary crewmember must be qualified or in training for qualification in that crew position, mission, and weapon system. Those crewmembers in a training status will accomplish weapon system operations and/or duties only under the supervision of a qualified instructor. **(T-3)**

2.6.1. Basic cybercrew qualified (BCQ) crewmembers have completed an evaluation and are qualified to perform basic crew duties on the CDA. BCQ crewmembers may perform primary crew duties on any training sortie and on missions (including unilateral training, joint training and exercises) when receiving Mission Qualification Training (MQT) or evaluations under the supervision of a qualified instructor in their respective crew position. **(T-3)**

2.6.2. Basic mission capable (BMC) crewmembers may perform primary crew duties on any training mission. The unit commander must determine the readiness of each BMC crewmember to perform primary crew duties. **(T-3)**

2.6.3. Mission ready (MR) crewmembers may perform primary crew duties in any position in which they maintain qualification, certification, currency and proficiency. **(T-3)**

2.6.4. Non-current or unqualified crewmembers may perform crew duties only on designated training or evaluation missions under the supervision of a qualified instructor. **(T-3)**

2.6.4.1. The Operations Group Commander (OG/CC), may authorize unqualified personnel to perform duties in non-operator crew positions (e.g., Distinguished Visitor (DV) visits) during execution under direct instructor supervision. This familiarization will only be conducted in permissive environments, and only when mission accomplishment is not impacted. **(T-3)**

2.7. New/Modified Equipment and/or Capabilities. Crewmembers not qualified and/or certified in the operation of significant new hardware and/or weapon system capabilities will not operate that hardware or perform any duties associated with that weapon system capability(s). Crewmembers not qualified or certified will work under the supervision of a current and qualified instructor unless otherwise specified by MAJCOM guidance. Non-Current events must be satisfied before the individual is considered certified/qualified (as applicable) to perform those events unsupervised. **(T-3)**

2.8. Crew Rest/Duty Period/Sortie Duration. Crew rest, crew duty period and crew augmentation will be IAW all applicable guidance with the following additional guidance:

2.8.1. Crew Rest. Crew rest is a minimum 12-hour non-duty period before the duty period begins to ensure the crewmember is adequately rested before performing a mission or mission-related duties. Crew rest is free time, and includes time for meals, transportation and rest. Rest is defined as a condition that allows an individual the opportunity to sleep. Each crewmember is individually responsible for ensuring they obtain sufficient rest during crew rest periods. **(T-3)**

2.8.2. Duty Period. The normal crew duty period is up to twelve (12) hours. **(T-3)**

2.8.3. Sortie. For planning purposes, the average sortie duration is six (6) hours. This does not include crew step and/or pre-mission brief, debrief and submitting Mission Reports (MISREP). **(T-3)**

2.9. Crew Scheduling. All crew members are responsible for maintaining awareness of scheduled sorties. **(T-3)**

Chapter 3

MISSION MATERIALS

3.1. Mission Resources. All resources used in the execution of AF CDA operational missions will be current and available to crews before each mission. This includes databases, mission folders, trackers, etc. and operator aids (Standard Operating Procedures, crew aids, etc.).

3.2. Crew Information Files (CIF).

3.2.1. The CIF is a library consisting of, at a minimum, a current read file and publications. Crewmembers will review CIF/Crew Bulletin before all missions, and update the CIF currency record with the latest CIF item number, date, and crewmember's initials. **(T-3)**

3.2.2. Electronic signatures or hard copy sign-off may be used on CIFs. **(T-3)**

3.2.3. Crewmembers delinquent in CIF review or joining a mission enroute will receive a CIF update from a primary crewmember counterpart executing the mission. **(T-3)**

3.3. Crew Bulletin (CB). Utilized primarily for crew notification, and included in Step Briefs. Items in the CB may include local procedures and policies concerning equipment and personnel generally not found in any other publications.

3.4. Crew Checklists/Aids.

3.4.1. Mission crewmembers will use all required technical orders for their assigned position. All crewmembers will have current hardcopy/softcopy technical orders for mission start-up, recovery and complex, critical, or time-sensitive tasks to be performed by the mission crewmembers. All technical orders for each crew mission position may be consolidated and centrally stored and maintained. **(T-3)**

3.4.2. Unit Standardization/Evaluation (Stan/Eval) will maintain the CIF library, listing current and authorized standard operating procedures, technical orders, crew aids, etc. **(T-3)**

3.4.3. All operators can provide mission material updates and/or inputs to Stan/Eval. For local materials, Stan/Eval will review for possible incorporation into mission materials. **(T-3)**

3.5. Mission Databases. The mission database (also known as the CDA database) is the unit's official record of events that occurred during operations. A separate dedicated database is used for training sorties. The purpose of the database is to maintain an accurate and detailed record of all significant events pertaining to operations occurring during each sortie. **(T-3)**

3.5.1. Units will maintain local databases to track and record events. **(T-3)**

3.5.2. The CDA-OC will input pertinent mission data into the mission database and the sortie database, both of which are contained within the CDA database. The CDA-OC will notify the CMS once mission data is complete. **(T-3)**

3.5.2.1. The CMS is responsible for content, accuracy, and timeliness of all inputs to mission-related information management portals/collaborative information sharing environments IAW with applicable directives, tasking, and policy. **(T-3)**

Chapter 4

MISSION PLANNING

4.1. Responsibilities. Individual crews, unit operations and analytical functions jointly share responsibility for mission planning. The CDA/OC is responsible for all tactical mission planning. Unit commanders may supplement mission planning requirements but will ensure an appropriate level of mission planning is conducted prior to each mission. **(T-3)**

4.1.1. Mission Planning Cell (MPC). If an MPC is utilized, the unit/DO or MPC Chief (MPCC) will determine the show time. **(T-3)**

4.1.1.1. The Squadron (SQ)/DO will ensure MPC is manned for each tasked mission through Crew Scheduling. **(T-3)**

4.1.1.2. The MPC can be tailored in size, manning, positions, and grade to meet mission planning requirements. **(T-3)**

4.2. Standard Operating Procedures (SOP). The unit/CC is the approval authority for unit standards. The Operations Group (OG)/CC may publish group standards. The OG Standardization and Evaluation office (OGV) will review all standards for compliance with AFI 17-series guidance. **(T-3)**

4.3. Mission Planning Guidelines.

4.3.1. Effective mission accomplishment requires thorough mission planning and preparation. Specific mission planning elements are addressed in Air Force Tactics, Techniques, and Procedures (AFTTP) 3-1.General Planning, AFTTP 3-1.CDA, Air Force Cyber Command (AFCYBER) & Joint Forces Headquarters-Cyber (JFHQ-C) AFCYBER Tactical Mission Planning, Briefing and Debriefing Guide, and any local crew aids. While not directive, these manuals are authoritative and useful in ensuring adequate mission planning and employment. **(T-3)**

4.3.2. The unit will provide adequate time and facilities for mission planning. Crews will accomplish sufficient planning to ensure successful mission accomplishment. Units will maintain facilities where all information and materials required for mission planning are available. All crews are required to receive a mission briefing prior to executing tasked missions. **(T-3)**.

4.3.3. The following mission information should be covered by the mission planners during planning: **(T-3)**.

4.3.3.1. Mission priorities **(T-3)**

4.3.3.2. Operational and tactical objectives **(T-3)**

4.3.3.3. Measures of performance **(T-3)**

4.3.3.4. Measures of effectiveness

4.3.3.5. Unit mission description (if applicable) **(T-3)**

4.3.3.6. Tasking order **(T-3)**

4.3.3.7. Significant rules (e.g., SPINS, ROE) **(T-3)**

4.3.3.8. Current weapon system status **(T-3)**

4.3.3.9. Threat data/current intelligence **(T-3)**

4.3.3.10. Critical information list (CIL), if applicable **(T-3)**

4.3.3.11. Signature list (provided by signature author) **(T-3)**

4.3.3.12. Contact list **(T-3)**

4.3.3.13. Emergency POCs **(T-3)**

4.3.3.14. Vulnerability/operating window **(T-3)**

4.3.3.15. Deconfliction plan (if applicable) **(T-3)**

4.3.3.16. Abort criteria and contingency plan **(T-3)**

4.3.4. Crisis Mission Planning (CMP). Crisis planning activities are similar to deliberate planning activities, but CMP is based on dynamic operations, active threats, and time sensitive real-world conditions. **(T-3)**

4.3.5. The Group/CC is the approval authority for immediate execution of crisis action /Ad-hoc tasking's utilizing standing AFIN-wide signatures, with crisis planning being conducted concurrently. **(T-3)**

4.4. Mission Planning Cell (MPC). The MPC, when employed, is responsible for providing mission crews the most current mission execution information derived from multiple agencies. They are responsible for conducting mission-planning activities and to produce, review, brief, and disseminate the Pre-Mission Briefing (PMB) and pertinent mission information to the operations crews for execution. All crewmembers must attend the pre-mission brief prior to executing the mission. **(T-3)**

4.4.1. The Pre-Mission Briefing (PMB). The PMB must be formally presented to the crew force at least one duty day prior to scheduled mission execution. All crewmembers, unless excused by unit/DO, must attend the pre-mission brief prior to executing the mission. Operators assigned to perform the tasked mission who did not attend the formal PMB must review the brief prior to working the mission. **(T-3)**

4.5. Mission Planning Cell Chief (MPCC). The MPCC will be appointed by the SQ/DO. The MPCC must be a 5 skill level, unless otherwise designated by SQ/DO. The MPCC will serve as the primary analyst for a single tasked mission and a liaison between sortie crews and supported units or tasking authority. **(T-3)**

4.5.1. The MPCC must plan adequate time to discuss required briefing items commensurate with the complexity of the mission and operator capabilities. **(T-3)**

4.5.1.1. Coordinate with the tasking authority on the SPINS and CTO for the integration of CDA into the cyber employment plan. **(T-3)**

4.5.1.2. Obtain CTO and "breakout" new mission information pertinent to the unit. **(T-3)**

4.5.1.3. Review and disseminate current intelligence information. **(T-3)**

4.5.1.4. Prepare and brief Pre-Mission Briefing. **(T-3)**

4.5.1.5. Prepare and attend sortie step briefs/debriefs. **(T-3)**

4.5.1.6. Collect and pass planning "Lessons Learned" to all MPC members and CDA units. **(T-3)**

4.5.1.7. Nominate and maintain Prioritized Intelligence Requirements (PIRs) and establish and refine associated Essential Elements of Information (EEIs). **(T-3)**

4.6. Signature Development will be conducted by a support element and integrated into mission, planning, research, and debrief to develop/refine mission signatures for weapon system employment. **(T-3)**

Chapter 5

MISSION EXECUTION

5.1. General Guidelines. The guidelines in this chapter contain the minimum requirements for mission execution. Units may develop supplemental baseline standards for mission execution. **(T-3)**

5.2. Crew Pre-Mission Preparations. Mission crews will perform, at a minimum, the following tasks prior to mission start:

5.2.1. Pre-Mission Arrival and Check-In. Each crewmember will report for their sortie at the scheduled time, ensuring they have sufficient crew rest. Sortie show time will allow sufficient time to accomplish all pre-mission activities. **(T-3)**

5.2.1.1. Go/No Go Validation. Prior to mission launch/start, the CMS will verify the mission crew is on-station and prepared to execute tasked missions and that individual crewmembers are current, qualified, and/or adequately supervised to perform operations and have reviewed CIF Volume 1, Part B prior to conducting operations. At a minimum, the unit Go/No-Go process will verify the following for all crewmembers, to include instructors and evaluators, scheduled to perform crew duties: **(T-3)**

5.2.1.2. Qualification/certification of each scheduled crewmember IAW AFI 17-2 CDA Volume 1, *Cyberspace Defense Analysis Training* and AFI 17-2 CDA Volume 2, *Air Force Cyberspace Defense Analysis (CDA) Standardization and Evaluation* for the crew position, mission, and duties they are scheduled to perform. Note: Crewmembers not qualified/certified and in training status will require instructor supervision to conduct crew duties. **(T-3)**

5.2.1.3. Currency and proficiency of each scheduled crewmember IAW AFI 17-2CDAV1 for the crew position, mission, and duties they are scheduled to perform. Note: Crewmembers not current in the crew position and/or mission will require instructor supervision to conduct crew duties until regaining currency. **(T-3)**

5.2.1.4. CIF Review. Crewmembers will review Volume I Part B, Current Read File of CIF, directly pertinent to the safe conduct of operations. Crewmembers will utilize Go No-Go procedures to verify review of the CIF. **(T-3)**

5.2.2. Crew Brief. Crewmembers will receive a step brief prior to stepping to the weapon system. The CDA-OC will ensure all crewmembers are briefed, at a minimum, on crew requirements and responsibilities, weapon system configurations/changes, CIF items/updates, Go/No-Go status, TTP updates, emergency action procedures, mission/training objectives, and any mission changes. Unit will adjust Step Brief as needed to ensure fulfillment of mission requirements. **(T-3)**

5.2.2.1. Unbriefed missions/events will not be executed. **(T-3)**

5.2.3. Mission Crew Resource Verification. Each crewmember will perform an inventory of all position mission resources, and notify the CMS if issues need to be addressed. **(T-3)**

5.2.4. System Status Verification. Prior to mission launch/start, the sortie CDA-OC, in coordination with mission assurance personnel, will verify the operational status of mission equipment, sensors, mission signatures, and report status to the CMS or unit/DO. **(T-3)**

5.2.4.1. If any required systems are NMC or PMC or are projected to be inoperable, the Cyberspace Mission Supervisor (CMS) or unit/DO will declare mission delay/cancelation/abort as appropriate IAW paragraph 5.3. **(T-3)**

5.3. CMS. Maintains command and control (C2) of CDA cybercrew operations and provides oversight for personnel conducting mission as well as enforcing policies and procedures to ensure successful mission accomplishment. The CMS directs/coordinates near real-time responses and timely reporting of operation disclosures in accordance with appropriate guidance. The CMS is responsible for understanding and executing Emergency Action Procedures, when applicable. CMS will:

5.3.1. Review and verify AFCTO taskings. **(T-3)**

5.3.2. Verify each crewmember's risk management level and sign off crewmembers on the Go/No-Go. **(T-3)**

5.3.3. Conduct the step brief. **(T-3)**

5.3.4. Establish and maintain C2 communications for coordination with external agencies/mission partners. CMS will report "On/Off Station" for all missions. **(T-3)**

5.3.5. Review and submit all CDA products to include MISREPs. **(T-3)**

5.3.6. Report mission outages (refer to local guidance). **(T-3)**

5.3.7. Coordinates any necessary crewmember changes. **(T-3)**

5.4. Launch/Mission/Abort Delay. Prior to mission start, recommend delay sortie start if the primary sensors or primary mission equipment are, or are projected to be, NMC or a minimum crew manning position(s) cannot be manned at sortie start time. The CMS will contact the Air Force Cyber Operations Center to inform them of the No-Go status. **(T-3)**

5.5. Contingency Considerations. The unit/DO may direct the non-support of the sortie or reallocate the mission to another AF CDA mission crew or location if available. **(T-3)**

Chapter 6

POST MISSION

6.1. Mission Assessment. CDA crewmembers will document mission highlights and deficiencies, keep mission statistics, record and archive essential mission data and assess mission performance. They will complete these actions as outlined by locally derived unit publications. **(T-3)**

6.2. Crew Debrief.

6.2.1. Each sortie will be debriefed by the CDA-OC assigned to that sortie. **(T-3)**

6.2.2. All crewmembers will attend the debrief. **(T-3)**

6.2.2.1. Attendance of specific crewmembers and other personnel (i.e., contractors, logistics support, etc.) should be based upon mission requirements and need-to-know. **(T-3)**

6.2.3. Debriefs will cover all aspects of the mission (planning, briefing and execution) and ensure all participants receive feedback through the development of Lessons Learned (LL) and Learning Points (LP). **(T-3)**

6.2.4. Crewmembers will not depart the duty area until completion of the debrief and are released by the CMS. **(T-3)**

6.3. Post Mission Duties.

6.3.1. System Readiness. All crewmembers will ensure weapon system is returned to a ready state as defined by unit/DO or CMS. **(T-3)**

6.3.2. Systems Refresh. All crewmembers will ensure workstations are restarted after each duty day is completed. It is the CDA-OC responsibility to ensure the sortie workstations are cleaned, sanitized, and restarted. **(T-3)**

6.4. Mission Report (MISREP). The CMS is responsible for receiving and disseminating timely, accurate, and correctly formatted reports IAW tasking authority guidance. **(T-3)**

6.4.1. MISREPs will be completed post-mission and prior to departing. **(T-3)**

6.4.2. The CDA-OC is responsible for providing the appropriate data regarding their mission area(s) for the MISREP and disseminating to the CMS. **(T-3)**

6.4.3. Local procedures/templates may be developed to ensure standardization of reporting. **(T-3)**

6.5. Product Dissemination. CMS will compiled and disseminated IAW local or tasking authority guidance. **(T-3)**

WILLIAM J. BENDER, Lt Gen, USAF
Chief of Information Dominance and Chief
Information Officer

Attachment 1

GLOSSARY OF REFERENCES AND SUPPORTING INFORMATION

References

Executive Order 9397, *Numbering System for Federal Accounts Relating to Individual Persons,* 30 November 1943, as amended by *Executive Order* 13478, Amendments to Executive Order 9397 Relating to Federal Agency Use of Social Security Numbers, November 18, 2008.

Privacy Act (PA) of 1947

Air Force (AF) Policy Directive (AFPD) 17-2, *Cyberspace Operations,* 12 April 2016

AFPD 14-2, *Intelligence Rules and Procedures,* 29 November 2007

AFI 17-2 CDA Volume 1, *Cyberspace Defense Analysis Training,* 27 April 2017

AFI 17-2 CDA Volume 2, *Air Force Cyberspace Defense Analysis (CDA) Standardization and Evaluation,* 27 April 2017

AFI 17-202V3, *Cyberspace Operations and Procedures,* 6 May 2015

AFI 10-701, *Operations Security (OPSEC),* 8 June 2011

AFI 10-712, *CDA Operations and Notice and Consent Process,* 17 December 2015

AFI 11-260, *Tactics Development Program,* 15 September 2011

AFI 11-415, *Weapons & Tactics Program,* 15 October 2014

AFI 14-104, *Oversight of Intelligence Activities,* 5 November 2014

AFI 33-332, *Air Force Privacy and Civil Liberties Program,* 12 January 2015

AFI 33-360, *Publications and Forms Management,* 1 December 2015

AFMAN 33-363, *Management of Records, Management of Records,* 1 March 2008, (*Incorporating Change* 2, 9 June 2016, *Certified Current* 21 July 2016).

Prescribed Forms

None

Adopted Forms

AF Form 679, *Air Force Publication Compliance Item Waiver Request/Approval*

AF Form 847, *Recommendation for Change of Publication*

Abbreviations and Acronyms

A— Analyst

AD— Active Duty

AF— Air Force

AFI— Air Force Instruction

AFMAN— Air Force Manual

AFCYBER— Air Force Cyber Command

AFPD— Air Force Policy Directive

AFRC— Air Force Reserve Command

AFRIMS— Air Force Records Information Management System

AFTTP— Air Force Tactics, Techniques and Procedures

ANG— Air National Guard

AOC— Air and Space Operations Center

AOR— Area of Responsibility

ARC— Air Reserve Component

BCQ— Basic Cybercrew qualified

BMC— Basic Mission Capable

C2— Command and Control

CB— Crew Bulletin

CDA— Cyber Defense Analysis

CIF— Crew Information File

CMP—Crisis Mission Planning

CMS—Cyber Mission Supervisor

CTO— Cyber Tasking Order

CO— Cyber Operator

COCOM— Combatant Command

DAF— Department of the Air Force

DCGS— Distributed Common Ground System

DIA— Defense Intelligence Agency

DO— Director of Operations

DRU— Direct Reporting Unit

DV—Distinguished Visitor

DVMS— Deployed Voice Monitoring System

EEI— Essential Elements of Information

FMC— Fully Mission Capable

FTU— Formal Training Unit

HAF— Headquarters Air Force

HHQ— Higher Headquarters

HQ— Headquarters

IAW—In Accordance With

JFHQ-C – Joint Forces Headquarters-Cyber

LL—Lessons Learned

LP— Learning Points

MAJCOM— Major Command

MISREPs—Mission Reports

MPC— Mission Planning Cell

MPPC—Mission Planning Cell Chief

MQT— Mission Qualification Training

MR— Mission Ready

NGB—National Guard Bureau

NMC— Non Mission Capable

NRT - Near—Real Time

OC— Operation Center

OCA— Original Classification Authority

OG—Operations Group

OGV—Operations Group and Evaluation Office

OPCON— Operational Control

OPLAN— Operational Plan

OPR— Office of Primary Responsibility

ORM— Operations Risk Management

PIR— Prioritized Intelligence Requirements

PLANORD— Planning Order

PMB – Pre-Mission Briefing

RDS—Records Disposition Schedule

RF—Radio Frequency

RFI— Request for Information

ROE— Rules of Engagement

SECDEF— Secretary of Defense

SDO— Senior Duty Officer

SME— Subject Matter Expert

SOF— Special Operations Forces

SOP—Standard Operating Procedures

SPINS— Special Instructions

Stan/Eval— Standardization/Evaluation

TIP— Tactic Improvement Proposal

TTP— Tactics, Techniques and Procedures

UHF—Ultra High Frequency

USAF— United States Air Force

VHF—Very High Frequency

W&T— Weapons and Tactics

WRA— Web Risk Assessment

Terms

Basic Mission Capable (BMC)— The status of CDA mission crewmembers who satisfactorily completed MQT, are qualified in the unit mission, but do not maintain MR status.

Mission Ready (MR)— The status of CDA mission crewmembers who satisfactorily completed MQT and maintain qualification and currency in the appropriate tasks and knowledge

required by this document.

Crew— The total complement of crewmembers required to operate a mission system and complete an assigned mission.

Crew Information File (CIF)— Files used to inform mission crewmembers on items of interest pertaining to the system and/or personnel. This

includes items such as changes in operating procedures, safety warnings, deployment procedures, software changes, etc.

Mission Qualification Training (MQT)— Training needed to qualify mission crewmembers to

perform their specific squadron (SQ) mission in an assigned position. This training is a prerequisite
for MR or BMC status.

BY ORDER OF THE
SECRETARY OF THE AIR FORCE

AIR FORCE INSTRUCTION 17-101

2 FEBRUARY 2017

Cyberspace

RISK MANAGEMENT FRAMEWORK
(RMF) FOR AIR FORCE
INFORMATION TECHNOLOGY (IT)

COMPLIANCE WITH THIS PUBLICATION IS MANDATORY

ACCESSIBILITY: Publications and forms are available for downloading or ordering on the e-Publishing website at **www.e-publishing.af.mil**.

RELEASABILITY: There are no releasability restrictions on this publication.

OPR: SAF/CIO A6ZC

Certified by: SAF/CIO A6Z
(Peter E. Kim, AF CISO)

Supersedes: AFI33-210, 23 December 2008

Pages: 49

This Air Force Instruction (AFI) implements Air Force Policy Directive (AFPD) 17-1, *Information Dominance Governance and Management,* 12 April 2016, AFPD 33-3, *Information Management*, 8 September, 2011, DoDI 8510.01, *Risk Management Framework (RMF) for DoD Information Technology (IT)*, 12 March 2014, and associated processes outlined on the AF RMF Knowledge Service (KS), for managing the life-cycle cybersecurity risk to Air Force Information Technology (IT) consistent with the Federal Information Security Modernization Act (FISMA) of 2014, DoDI 8500.01, *Cybersecurity*, 14 March 2014, and DoD Directive 8000.01, *Management of the Department of Defense Information Enterprise*, 10 February 2009. This instruction is consistent with Chairman Joint Chiefs of Staff Instruction (CJCSI) 6510.01F, *Information Assurance (IA) and Support to Computer Network Defense (CND)*. Direct questions, comments, recommended changes, or conflicts to this publication through command channels using the AF Form 847, *Recommendation for Change of Publication*, to SAF/CIO A6.

This publication applies to all military and civilian AF personnel, members of the AF Reserve Command (AFRC), Air National Guard (ANG), third-party governmental employee and contractor support personnel in accordance with appropriate provisions contained in memoranda support agreements and AF contracts.

The authorities to waive requirements in this publication are identified with a Tier number (T-0, T-1, T-2, T-3) following the compliance statement. See AFI 33-360, *Publications and Forms Management*, Table 1.1 for a description of the authorities associated with the Tier numbers. Submit requests for waivers through the chain of command to the appropriate Tier waiver approval authority, or alternately, to the Publication office of primary responsibility (OPR) for non-tiered compliance items. Send any supplements to this publication to SAF/CIO A6 for review, coordination, and approval prior to publication. Unless otherwise noted, the SAF/CIO A6 is the waiver authority to policies contained in this publication. Ensure all records created as a result of processes prescribed in this publication are maintained in accordance with (IAW) AFMAN 33-363, *Management of Records*, and disposed of IAW Air Force Records Disposition Schedule (RDS) located in the Air Force Records Information Management System (AFRIMS).

SUMMARY OF CHANGES

This document is substantially changed and must be reviewed in its entirety. This instruction reissues, renames, supersedes, and rescinds AFI 33-210, *Air Force Certification and Accreditation Program,* to AFI 17-101, *Risk Management Framework for Air Force Information Technology.* This directive establishes the Risk Management Framework (RMF) for AF IT, establishes associated cybersecurity policy, and assigns responsibilities for executing and maintaining the RMF. The RMF replaces the DoD Information Assurance Certification and Accreditation Process (DIACAP) and manages the life-cycle cybersecurity risk to AF IT.

Chapter 1

PROGRAM OVERVIEW

1.1. Purpose. This AFI provides implementation instructions for the Risk Management Framework (RMF) methodology for Air Force (AF) Information Technology (IT) according to AFPD 17-1, *Information Dominance Governance and Management*, and AFI 17-130, *Air Force Cybersecurity Program Management*, which is only one component of cybersecurity.

1.1.1. The RMF incorporates strategy, policy, awareness/training, assessment, continuous monitoring, authorization, implementation, and remediation.

1.1.2. The RMF aligns with SAF/CIO A6's AF Information Dominance Flight Plan key concept of increasing cybersecurity of AF information systems; therefore, robust risk assessment and management is required.

1.1.3. The RMF process encompasses life cycle risk management to determine and manage the residual cybersecurity risk to the AF created by the vulnerabilities and threats associated with objectives in military, intelligence, and business operations.

1.1.4. Effective implementation and resultant residual risk associated with security controls implementation is assessed and mitigated, aligns with DoDI 8510.01, and as documented in the RMF security authorization package for AF IT.

1.1.5. Discrete classes of systems (i.e., AF financial systems) are subject to additional requirements contained in Attachment 3 to this document. Guidance contained in Attachment 3 are intended to supplement, but not replace, the policy limits articulated in this Instruction.

1.2. Applicability.

1.2.1. This publication is binding on all military, civilian and contract employees, and other individuals or organizations as required by binding agreement or obligation with the Department of the Air Force, who develop, acquire, deliver, use, operate, support, or manage AF IT. This publication applies to all networked or standalone IT used to receive, process, store, display, or transmit AF information (or Government information where the AF agreed to manage the information/infrastructure), as well as DoD partnered systems where it is agreed that DoD standards are followed. AF IT (see Figure 1.1) includes but is not limited to: information systems (IS) (major applications and enclaves), platform information technology (PIT) (PIT systems, PIT subsystems, and PIT products), IT services (Internal & External), and IT products (software, hardware, and applications).

1.2.2. This AFI does not apply to the protection of Sensitive Compartmented Information (SCI) systems or intelligence, surveillance, reconnaissance mission and mission support systems or higher authoritative guidance governing Special Access Program (SAP) systems.

1.2.3. Authority for AF space systems rests with AF Space Command (AFSPC) as delegated by United States Strategic Command (USSTRATCOM). AF space systems follow AF cybersecurity policy and processes; where exceptions exist, this Instruction is annotated accordingly. NOTE: Space systems supporting more than one DoD Component will follow cybersecurity policy and guidance in DoDI 8581.01, *Information Assurance (IA) Policy for Space Systems Used by the Department of Defense.*

1.2.4. For IT not centrally managed or has yet to be assigned an Authorizing Official (AO), the unit responsible for ownership or operation of the IT shall assign duties for the minimum RMF relevant roles (see Table 2.1) required to comply with RMF. The duties shall include the roles and responsibilities for reporting, oversight, and risk management to the AF.

Figure 1.1. Air Force IT Categories.

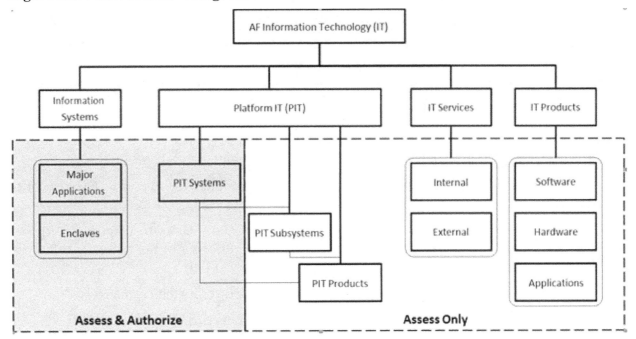

1.3. Objectives.

1.3.1. The RMF replaces the DIACAP and manages the life-cycle cybersecurity risk to AF IT. The RMF provides a disciplined and structured process to perform AF IT security and risk management activities and to integrate those activities into the system development life cycle. The RMF changes the traditional focus of certification and accreditation (C&A) as a static, procedural activity to a more dynamic approach to more effectively manage mission and cybersecurity risks in diverse environments of complex, evolving, and sophisticated cyber threats and vulnerabilities.

1.3.2. The RMF ensures AF IT assets are assessed for cybersecurity risk to the AF, the discovered weaknesses are documented in a plan of action and milestones (POA&M) to mitigate residual risk, and an AO, supported by the RMF team members, identified at Table 2.1, accepts the risk to the AO's area of responsibility, IAW AFPD 16-14, *Security Enterprise Governance,* and DoDI 8510.01.

Chapter 2

ROLES AND RESPONSIBILITIES

2.1. Secretary of the Air Force, Office of Information Dominance and Chief Information Officer (SAF/CIO A6). The SAF/CIO A6 will:

2.1.1. Appoint the Chief Information Security Officer (CISO) who develops, implements, maintains, and enforces the AF Cybersecurity Program.

2.1.2. Maintain visibility of the cybersecurity posture for AF IT through automated tools or designated repositories in support of DoD CIO and appointed AOs. **(T-0)**

2.1.3. Provide guidance to organizations on how to implement solutions for operational requirements in support of established National, DoD, Joint Chiefs of Staff (JCS), or AF security controls for IT and remain within established risk tolerance levels. **(T-0)**

2.1.4. Appoint AOs in coordination with the appropriate Mission Area Owner (MAO).

2.1.5. Ensure an Information System Owner (ISO) is appointed for all AF IT.

2.1.6. Appoint the AF Chief Architect with responsibility for the AF Cybersecurity Architecture IAW AFI 17-140, *Air Force Architecting*.

2.1.7. Define cybersecurity performance measurements and metrics to identify enterprise-wide cybersecurity trends and status of mitigation efforts, IAW NIST SP 800-55, *Performance Measurement Guide for Information Security*. **(T-0)**

2.1.8. Be responsible for the security controls implemented across the IT enterprise.

2.2. Administrative Assistant to the Secretary of the Air Force (SAF/AA).

2.2.1. Works with the CISO to oversee the establishment of risk tolerance and security controls for IT owned by Headquarters Air Force (HAF) organizations without a functional CIO (HAF Portfolio).

2.2.2. Provides guidance to organizations on how to implement solutions for operational requirements for the HAF Portfolio.

2.2.3. Maintains visibility of the cybersecurity posture of HAF Portfolio IT through automated assessment and authorization tools.

2.3. Secretary of the Air Force for Acquisition (SAF/AQ).

2.3.1. Acquires all AF electronic systems through organic programs within the AF, commercial-off-the-shelf (COTS) systems, or non-developmental item (NDI) programs. The PM shall pursue comprehensive integrated risk analysis throughout the life cycle of all programs and shall prepare and maintain a risk management plan.

2.3.2. Works with the CISO to oversee the establishment of risk tolerance and security controls for AF IT. Provides guidance to organizations on how to implement solutions for operational requirements.

2.3.3. Ensures all cyber /IT security controls are translated into security requirements via systems security engineering and are written into the System Requirement Document (SRD) on all acquisitions.

2.3.4. Ensures system security engineering is accomplished through the acquisition process for all new and upgrade capability developments.

2.4. Deputy Chief of Staff, Intelligence, Surveillance, and Reconnaissance (AF/A2).

2.4.1. Maintains visibility of the cybersecurity posture of AF SCI and the DoD portion of the Intelligence Mission Area (DIMA) IT through automated assessment and authorization tools.

2.4.2. Oversees the establishment of risk tolerance and baseline security controls for AF SCI and DIMA IT. Consults with SAF/A6 CISO as appropriate. Provides RMF implementation guidance to AF ISR systems and network organizations.

2.5. Chief Information Security Officer (CISO), SAF/CIO A6Z. Will develop, implement, maintain, and enforce the AF Cybersecurity Program and the RMF process, roles, and responsibilities. The CISO will advocate for any budgets associated with duties below and advocate for AF-wide cybersecurity solutions through the planning, programming, budget and execution process on behalf of the SAF/CIO A6. As a CISO, the role requires individuals be a DoD official (O-7 or SES at a minimum) and a United States citizen. **(T-1)** The CISO will:

2.5.1. Complete training and maintain cybersecurity certifications IAW AFMAN 17-1303, *Cybersecurity Workforce Improvement Program.* **(T-1)**

2.5.2. Monitor, evaluate, and provide advice to the SAF/CIO A6 regarding AF cybersecurity posture.

2.5.3. In coordination with the SAF/CIO A6 and AOs, ensure the cybersecurity risk posture, risk tolerance levels, and risk acceptance decisions for AF IT meet mission and business needs, IAW Commander, USSTRATCOM, 24 AF/CC, and AFI 10-1701, *Command and Control* (C2) *for Cyberspace Operations,* while also minimizing the operations and maintenance burden on the organization.

2.5.4. Perform as the Security Control Assessor (SCA) or appoint SCAs.

2.5.5. Provide guidance and direction on Agent of the Security Control Assessor (ASCA) establishment and licensing in support of RMF requirements. **(T-1)**

2.5.6. Oversee establishment and enforcement of the AF RMF, roles, and responsibilities; review approval thresholds and milestones within the RMF. **(T-1)**

2.5.7. Chair the Air Force Risk Management Council (AFRMC). **(T-1)**

2.5.8. Participate in Federal, Joint, DoD, and AF cybersecurity and RMF technical working groups and forums (e.g., Defense Information Assurance Security Accreditation Working Group (DSAWG)).

2.5.9. Adjudicate IT determinations, in coordination with the AFRMC, when a conflict in the IT determination process is identified. **(T-1)**

2.5.10. Appoint AF members to the DoD RMF TAG.

2.5.11. Review and approve Privacy Impact Assessments (PIAs) submitted IAW AFI 33-332, *The AF Privacy and Civil Liberties Program*. The approval of the PIA cannot be delegated. **(T-1)**

2.5.12. Approve national security system (NSS) designations for AF IT. **(T-1)**

2.5.13. Ensure AF RMF guidance is posted to the AF Component Workspace portion of the DoD Knowledge Service (KS) and is consistent with DoD policy and guidance.

2.6. Authorizing Official (AO). The AO is the official with the authority responsible for accepting a level of risk for a system balanced with mission requirements, except for IT with unmitigated "Very High" and "High" risk. The AO is the only person with authority to grant authorization decisions within their area of responsibility. All AOs have the flexibility in augmenting, executing, and implementing RMF for systems in their AOR. For example, AOs can create a community-specific guidebook for better clarifying guidance. AOs will:

2.6.1. Be a DoD official (O-7 or SES at a minimum) and a U.S. citizen. **(T-1)**

2.6.2. Complete training and certification requirements IAW AFMAN 17-1303. **(T-1)**

2.6.3. Be appointed by SAF/CIO A6, in coordination with the appropriate MAO. The appointment grants authority to authorize IT as defined in the AO appointment memo.

2.6.4. Advocate for cybersecurity-related positions in accordance with DoDI 8500.01, **(T-0)** AFI 17-130, and AFMAN 17-1303. **(T-1)**

2.6.5. Ensure an Information System Owner (ISO) (i.e., the owner, operator, maintainer of the IT) is appointed prior to issuing an authorization decision. **(T-1)**

2.6.6. Ensure ISOs participate throughout the RMF process and understand the risk imposed on the mission due to operating the IT.

2.6.7. Ensure verification through the AF Ports, Protocols, and Services (PPS) Office (**af.pps@us.af.mil**) that Internet protocols, data services, and associated ports (internal and external) of the system/enclave comply with the requirements outlined in DoDI 8551.01 *Ports, Protocols, and Services Management (PPSM)*. **(T-0)**

2.6.8. Assist the SAF/CIO A6 in providing guidance to organizations on how to implement solutions for operational requirements exceeding the established National, DoD, JCS, or AF baseline controls for IT.

2.6.9. Render authorization decisions that balance mission needs with security concerns for IT within the AO's area of responsibility. The Authorization Decision Documentation will be digitally signed and generated via Enterprise Mission Assurance Support Service (eMASS), except PIT. Any exceptions to or conditions of the authorization decision must be articulated within the Authorization Decision Document. **(T-0)**

2.6.10. Review the security assessment report (SAR), risk assessment report (RAR), and POA&M to ensure there is a clearly defined course of action, see also NIST SP 800-30, *Guide for Conducting Risk Assessments*. An AO may downgrade or revoke an authorization decision at any time, if risk conditions or concerns so warrant. **(T-0)**

2.6.11. Review and approve the security assessment plan (SAP), the security plan, and system-level information security continuous monitoring (ISCM) strategy.

2.6.12. Ensure all AF IT comply with DoD and AF connection approval processes, see **Chapter 4**.

2.6.13. Not delegate authorization decision authority (i.e., to formally accept risk for a system). **(T-0)**

NOTE: Appointment letters and AO Boundaries are located on the AF RMF KS.

2.7. Air Force Enterprise Authorizing Official (AF Enterprise AO). The AF Enterprise AO is the only authority permitted to grant an Approval to Connect (ATC) to the Air Force Information Networks (AFIN). The Enterprise AO may delegate this authority to appropriate deputies with concurrence of the SAF/CIO A6. In addition to the AO responsibilities in paragraph 2.6 above, the Enterprise AO will:

2.7.1. Establish acceptable security controls and risk tolerance for connecting to the AFIN and provide guidance to implementing organizations to mitigate risk commensurate with established risk tolerance.

2.7.2. Review the Security Authorization Package, as a minimum, for all requests to connect to the AFIN and assess the impact to enterprise community risk. **(T-1)**

2.7.3. Render authorization decisions in the form of an authorization to operate (ATO) for AF systems not falling under another AO. Render AFIN connection decisions in the form of an ATC (see **Chapter 4**) for non-AF systems and for AF systems falling under another AO. **(T-1)**

2.7.4. The Enterprise AO or designee will expediently respond to urgent/emergency requests to connect to the AFIN.

2.7.5. See AFI 17-130, for additional information in support of this position.

2.8. AO Designated Representative (AODR). The AODR will:

2.8.1. Be appointed by the AO, and at a minimum, be an O-5 or GS-14. Appointments will be in writing (to include duties and responsibilities) to support the RMF. Digital signatures are authorized for appointment letters. **(T-1)**

2.8.2. The AODR may be supplemented with contractor support, however contractors are not permitted to make decisions on behalf of the government and may only provide advice and guidance.

2.8.3. Perform responsibilities as assigned by the AO. The AODR may perform any and all duties of an AO except for accepting risk by issuing an authorization decision.

2.8.4. Complete AO training and maintain cybersecurity certifications consistent with duties and responsibilities of an AO and IAW AFMAN 17-1303. **(T-1)**

2.8.5. Provide recommendations to the AO to render authorization decisions based on input from the SCA, ISO, PM, and other AOs and AODRs.

2.9. Security Control Assessor (SCA). The SCA will:

2.9.1. Be appointed by the CISO and will be at least an O-4 or GS-13 with the authority and responsibility for the assessment determination within their assigned area of responsibility.

2.9.2. Complete training and maintain appropriate cybersecurity certification IAW AFMAN 17-1303. It is highly recommended SCAs complete both the AO training module and attain the Committee on National Security Systems Instruction (CNSSI) 4016, *National Information Assurance Training Standard for Risk Analysts,* certificate for supplemental training. **(T-1)**

2.9.3. Develop the SAP and ensure its integration into the program office's Test and Evaluation Master Plan (TEMP) IAW DoDI 5000.02, *Operation of the Defense Acquisition System.* **(T-0)**

2.9.4. Prepare the SAR documenting the issues, findings, and recommendations from the security control assessment, and reassess remediated controls, as required. **(T-0)**

2.9.5. Periodically assess security controls employed within and inherited by the IT IAW the Information Security Continuous Monitoring strategy. **(T-0)**

2.10. Security Controls Assessor Representative (SCAR). This position may be an organic or contracted resource. The SCAR works with the PM, ISSM, ISSO, and RMF team to assess security controls for the SCA. The SCAR will:

2.10.1. Complete training and maintain appropriate cybersecurity certification IAW AFMAN 17-1303. It is recommended SCARs also complete the AO training module and attain the CNSSI No. 4016 certificate for supplemental training. **(T-1)**

2.10.2. Serve as an active member of the RMF team from its inception, to assist with planning of cybersecurity requirements. The SCAR ensures security controls are implemented IAW the security plan and are assessed IAW the SAP. **(T-0)**

2.10.3. Validate assessment results from others' (e.g., ASCA or ISSM) hands-on, comprehensive evaluations of the technical and non-technical security controls for the IT, determine the degree to which the IT satisfies the applicable security controls.

2.10.4. Should the SCAR be a contractor, the SCAR is not permitted to make decisions on behalf of the government but can only provide advice and guidance.

2.11. Agent of the Security Controls Assessor (ASCA). The ASCA is a licensed 3rd-party agent assisting in assessment activities and provides an independent report for the SCA. This position cannot make decisions on behalf of the government but can only provide advice and guidance. The ASCA will:

2.11.1. Achieve and maintain an ASCA license per the *AF and Space ASCA Licensing Guide.* **(T-0)**

2.11.2. Respond to PM, ISO, SCAR, SCA, and AO requests for information regarding their respective systems.

2.11.3. Perform comprehensive evaluation of the technical and non-technical security controls for the IT, determine the degree to which the IT satisfies the applicable security controls, and provide mitigation recommendations.

2.11.4. Perform assessment procedures for each applicable security control as outlined in the DoD RMF KS. **(T-0)**

2.11.5. Meet the intent of RMF independence between the PM or ISO and the individuals performing security control assessments; the ASCA reports only to the SCA.

2.11.6. The ASCA will not be part of the development team or program office. The PM or ISO provides funding for organizations or contractors to perform ASCA responsibilities; the PM or ISO does not provide direction or oversight to organizations or contractors in support of ASCA responsibilities.

2.11.7. All ASCA agreements must include safeguards to prevent a conflict of interests with the development team.

2.12. Information System Owners (ISO). Official responsible for the overall procurement, development, integration, modification, and operation and maintenance of AF IT. **(T-1)** An ISO is appointed and performs all PM roles and responsibilities when a PM is not assigned. For AF-wide systems (e.g., AFNET and LOGMOD), the ISO is appointed by the HAF/SAF 3-letter responsible for the capability. For MAJCOM-level or base-level IT, to include base enclaves, and PIT, the appropriate MAJCOM 2-letter appoints the ISO. **(T-1)** No further appointment is required. This ISO role is not the same as the TEMPEST ISO. The ISO will:

2.12.1. Identify the requirement for the IT and request funds to operate and maintain the IT in order to assure mission effectiveness. **(T-2)**

2.12.2. Ensure, with coordination of the PM staff, the development, maintenance, and tracking of the security plan for assigned IT. **(T-1)**

2.12.3. Ensure, with coordination of the PM staff, the development of an ISCM strategy to monitor the effectiveness of all security controls employed within or inherited by the system, and to monitor any proposed or actual changes to the system and its environment of operation. **(T-0)**

2.12.4. Report the security status of the IT including the effectiveness of security controls employed within and inherited by the system to the AO and other appropriate organizational officials on an ongoing basis in accordance with the ISCM strategy.

2.12.5. Decide, in coordination with the Information Owner (IO)/Steward, who has access to the system (and what types of privileges or access rights) and ensure system users and support personnel receive the requisite security training. **(T-2)**

2.12.6. Inform, based on guidance from the SCA and AO, appropriate organizational officials to conduct the Authorize and Assess process or the Assess Only process; ensure the necessary resources are available for the effort, and provide the required IT access, information, and documentation to the SCA.

2.12.7. Conduct the initial remediation actions on security controls based on the findings and recommendations of the SAR and work with the SCA to reassess remediated controls.

2.12.8. Ensure the POA&M is developed for all identified weaknesses and the appropriate steps to mitigate those weaknesses are identified. Take appropriate steps to reduce or eliminate weaknesses, then generate the security authorization package and submit the package to the SCA for assessment. **(T-0)**

2.12.9. Ensure open POA&M items are updated and closed in a timely manner. **(T-2)**

2.12.10. Ensure consolidated RMF documentation is maintained for systems with instances at multiple locations.

2.12.11. Thoroughly review the security controls assessment and risk assessment results before submitting the security authorization package to the AO, ensuring the system's cybersecurity posture satisfactorily supports mission, business, and budgetary needs (i.e., indicates the mission risk is acceptable).

2.12.12. Ensure, with the assistance of the ISSM, and coordination with the PM staff, the system is deployed and operated according to the approved security plan and the authorization package (i.e., the AO's authorization decision). **(T-0)**

2.13. Program Manager (PM). The ISO is assigned the PM duties when no PM is assigned. The PM will:

2.13.1. Identify, implement, and ensure full integration of cybersecurity into all phases of the acquisition, upgrade, or modification programs, including initial design, development, testing, fielding, operation, and sustainment IAW AFI 63-101, *Integrated Life Cycle Management,* and DoDI 8510.01, the *DoD Program Manager's Guidebook for Integrating the Cybersecurity Risk Management Framework (RMF) into the System Acquisition Lifecycle.* **(T-0)**

2.13.2. Ensure the Program Management Office (PMO) is resourced to support information system security engineering (ISSE) requirements and security technical assessments of the IT for the SCA's recommendation, the AOs authorization decision, and other security-related assessments (e.g., Financial Improvement and Audit Readiness IT testing, Inspector General audits). **(T-1)**

2.13.3. Ensure cybersecurity-related positions are assigned in accordance with Table 2.1 and AFMAN 17-1303. **(T-1)**

2.13.4. Appoint an ISSM, IAW DoDI 8510.01, for the program office and ensure the ISSM is certified IAW AFMAN 17-1303. **(T-0)**

2.13.5. Ensure the IT is registered IAW AFI 17-110, *Air Force Information Technology Portfolio Management and Investment Review.* **(T-1)**

2.13.6. Develop and maintain a cybersecurity strategy for IT IAW AFMAN 17-1402, *Air Force Clinger-Cohen Act (CCA) Compliance Guide*, and AFI 63-101/20-101. **(T-1)**

2.13.7. Ensure applicable Cyber Tasking Orders (CTO) are received and acted upon per the CTO directions. **(T-1)**

2.13.8. Ensure periodic reviews, testing, or assessment of assigned IT are conducted at least annually, and IAW the ISCM strategy.

2.13.9. Ensure operational systems maintain a current ATO and recommend to the AO that systems without a current authorization are identified for removal from operation. **(T-1)**

2.13.10. Ensure all system changes are approved through a configuration management process, are assessed for cybersecurity impacts, and coordinated with the SCA, AO, and other affected parties, such as IOs/Stewards and AOs of interconnected boundaries.

2.13.11. Track and implement the corrective actions identified in the POA&M, in order to provide visibility and status to the ISO, IO, AO, and CISO. **(T-0)**

2.13.12. Report security incidents to stakeholder organizations and the SCA. Conduct root cause analysis for incidents and develop corrective action plans as input to the POA&M.

2.13.13. Ensure a PIA is completed (DD Form 2930) for IT that process and/or store Personal Identifiable Information (PII)/Personal Health Information (PHI) IAW AFI 33-332, *Air Force Privacy and Civil Liberties Program.* **(T-1)**

2.14. Unit Communications Squadron Commander (CS/CC). Serves as the PM or ISO for the base enclave and performs duties IAW DoDI 5000.02 and AFI 17-130.

2.15. Information System Security Manager (ISSM). The ISSM is the primary cybersecurity technical advisor to the AO, PM, and ISO. For base enclaves, the ISSM manages the installation cybersecurity program, typically as a function of the Wing Cybersecurity Office. That program ISSM may also serve as the system ISSM for the enclave and reports to the CS/CC as the PM for the base enclave. The ISSM will:

2.15.1. Ensure the integration of cybersecurity into and throughout the lifecycle of the IT on behalf of the AO. **(T-0)**

2.15.2. Complete and maintain required cybersecurity certification IAW AFMAN 17-1303. Individuals in this position must be U.S. citizens. **(T-0)**

2.15.3. Ensure all AF IT cybersecurity-related documentation is current and accessible to properly authorized individuals. **(T-1)**

2.15.4. Support the PM or ISO in maintaining connection (ATC) and authorization (ATO) approvals and provide support to the PM or ISO in implementing corrective actions identified in the POA&M.

2.15.5. Coordinate, with the PM and AO staffs, development of an ISCM strategy and monitor any proposed or actual changes to the system and its environment.

2.15.6. Continuously monitor the IT and environment for security-relevant events, assess proposed configuration changes for potential impact to the cybersecurity posture, and assess the quality of security controls implementation against performance indicators such as security incidents, feedback from external inspection agencies, exercises, and operational evaluations. **(T-0)**

2.15.7. Ensure cybersecurity-related events or configuration changes that impact AF IT authorization or adversely impact the security posture are formally reported to the AO and other affected parties, such as IOs and stewards and AOs of interconnected IT.

2.15.8. Appoint Information System Security Officers (ISSOs) and provide oversight to ensure ISSOs follow established cybersecurity policies and procedures IAW DoDI 8500.01. (NOTE: ISSO appointments are not required if the ISSM has purview over a small amount of IT, but ISSO appointments are advisable when the ISSM has purview over multiple IT). **(T-0)**

2.15.9. Ensure all ISSOs and privileged users receive necessary technical training and obtain cybersecurity certification IAW AFMAN 17-1301, *Computer Security (COMPUSEC)*, AFMAN 17-1303 and maintain proper clearances IAW DoDI 8500.01. **(T-0)**

2.15.10. Ensure the AF IT is acquired, documented, operated, used, maintained, and disposed of properly and IAW DoDI 5000.02 and DoDI 8510.01. **(T-0)**

2.16. Information System Security Officer (ISSO). The ISSO is responsible for ensuring the appropriate operational security posture is maintained for assigned IT. The ISSM will take on these responsibilities should no ISSO be assigned. This includes the following activities related to maintaining situational awareness and initiating actions to improve or restore cybersecurity posture. ISSOs (formerly system-level IA Officers) will:

2.16.1. Implement and enforce all AF cybersecurity policies, procedures, and countermeasures. **(T-1)**

2.16.2. Complete and maintain required cybersecurity certification IAW AFMAN 17-1303. Individuals in this position must be U.S. citizens. **(T-0)**

2.16.3. Ensure all users have the requisite security clearances and need-to-know, complete annual cybersecurity training, and are aware of their responsibilities before being granted access to the IT according to AFMAN 17-1301. **(T-1)**

2.16.4. Maintain all authorized user access control documentation IAW the applicable AF Records Information Management System (AFRIMS). **(T-1)**

2.16.5. Ensure software, hardware, and firmware complies with appropriate security configuration guidelines (e.g., Security Technical Implementation Guides (STIGs)/Security Requirement Guides (SRG)). **(T-1)**

2.16.6. Ensure proper configuration management procedures are followed prior to implementation and contingent upon necessary approval. Coordinate changes or modifications with the system-level ISSM, SCA, and/or the Wing Cybersecurity office. **(T-1)**

2.16.7. Initiate protective or corrective measures, in coordination with the security manager, when a security incident or vulnerability is discovered. **(T-3)**

2.16.8. Report security incidents or vulnerabilities to the system-level ISSM and wing cybersecurity office according to AFI 17-130. **(T-2)**

2.16.9. Initiate exceptions, deviations, or waivers to cybersecurity requirements. **(T-1)**

2.17. Information Systems Security Engineer (ISSE). The ISSE is an individual, group, or organization responsible for conducting information system security engineering activities. ISSE captures and refines information security requirements and ensures the requirements are effectively integrated into IT products and information systems through purposeful security architecting, design, development, and configuration. Reference DoDI 5000.02, and NIST SP 800-160, *Systems Security Engineering - A Multidisciplinary Approach to Building Trustworthy Resilient Systems*, for additional details on systems engineering and information systems engineering processes. The ISSE traces security controls (which are high-level cybersecurity capability needs), with the RMF team, to the actual system security requirements documented in the acquisition process (i.e., many security requirements are derived from security controls). The ISSE will:

2.17.1. Employ best practices when implementing security controls, including software engineering methodologies, system/security engineering principles, secure design, secure architecture, and secure coding techniques.

2.17.2. Coordinate their security-related activities with the information security architect, ISSO, ISO, and common control provider.

2.17.3. Complete training and maintain certification IAW AFI 17-1303. Personnel performing any IA Workforce System Architecture and Engineering (IASAE) specialty function(s) (one or more functions) at any level must be certified to the highest level function(s) performed. (T-0)

2.18. Information Owner (IO)/Steward. An organizational official with statutory, management, or operational authority for specified information and the responsibility for establishing the policies and procedures governing its generation, classification, collection, processing, dissemination, and disposal as defined in CNSSI No. 4009. The IO/Steward will:

2.18.1. Provide input to the ISO regarding security requirements and security controls for the IT where the information is processed, stored, or transmitted. (T-2)

2.18.2. Establish the rules for appropriate use and protection of the information, during generation, collection, processing, dissemination, and disposal and retain that responsibility even when the information is shared with or provided to other organizations. (T-1)

2.18.3. Provide input to ISOs on the security controls selection (e.g., during system categorization and security controls tailoring) and on the derived security requirements for the systems where the information is processed, stored, or transmitted (A single IS, PIT system, or PIT subsystem may contain information from multiple IO/stewards.) (T-1)

2.19. MAJCOM Cybersecurity Office or Function. The MAJCOM Cybersecurity Office or Function will:

2.19.1. Develop, implement, oversee, and maintain a MAJCOM cybersecurity program that adheres to cybersecurity architecture, requirements, objectives, policies, processes, and procedures.

2.19.2. Tracks and reports Federal Information Security Modernization Act of 2014 (FISMA) metrics to SAF/CIO A6 Cybersecurity on a monthly, quarterly, and annual basis as required via Enterprise Information Technology Data Repository / Information Technology Investment Portfolio System (EITDR/ITIPS) or DoD Cyberscope (DCS).

2.20. User Representative (UR). The User Representative is the individual or organization that represents operational and functional requirements of the user community for a particular system during the RMF process. The UR supports the security controls selection, implementation, and assessment to ensure user community needs are met. While this role is not mandatory, it is highly recommended this role be used. The individuals in this role understand the operating environment, mission criticality, reliability and survivability requirements, etc., of the system.

2.21. Additional Responsibilities. Additional responsibilities and authorities relevant to many of the roles listed above are contained in the attachments.

Table 2.1. AF RMF Appointment Matrix.

Role	Appointed/ Identified By	Rank Minimum	Reference(s)
SAF/CIO A6[+]	SecAF (established)	O-9	HAF MD1-26
CISO	SAF-CIO A6	O-7 / SES	DoDI 8500.01
MAO	Identified	O-7 / SES	AFPD 16-14
AO*[+]	SAF-CIO A6	O-7 / SES	AFI 17-130
AODR	AO	O-5 / GS-14	AFI 17-130
SCA*[+]	CISO	O-4 / GS-13	AFI 17-130
PM[+]	For programs of record, Service Acquisition Executive (SAE) (as applicable); otherwise, ISO performs duties.	Any government official	DoDI 5000.02
ISO*[+]	For programs of record, Service Acquisition Executive (SAE) (as applicable); otherwise, HAF/SAF 3-letter or MAJCOM 2-letter (as applicable)	Any	AFI 17-101
IO/Steward	Identified by the ISSM	Any	DoDI 8500.01, NIST SP 800-37r1
ISSE[+]	PM	Any	DoDI 8510.01
ISSM*[+]	PM or ISO	Any	DoDI 8510.01
ISSO[+]	ISSM	Any	AFI 17-130
UR	ISO	Any	DoDI 8510.01

* Denotes minimum system-level RMF positions

+ Denotes additional responsibilities and authorities assigned in Attachments

2.22. Cybersecurity Forums. The AF leverages existing DoD and AF governance bodies (e.g., Air Force Security Enterprise Executive Board (AFSEEB), Information Technology Governance Executive Board (ITGEB)) to discuss cybersecurity risk topics and make organizational and mission area risk decisions. This Instruction does not define the scope or responsibilities of these existing bodies. The following forums provide focused management and oversight of the AF Cybersecurity Program.

2.22.1. AF Cybersecurity Technical Advisory Group (AFCTAG). The AFCTAG provides technical cybersecurity subject matter experts (SMEs) from across the MAJCOMs and functional communities to facilitate the management, oversight, and execution of the AF

Cybersecurity Program.   The AFCTAG examines cybersecurity-related issues common across AF entities and provides recommendations to the CISO and DSAWG on changes to the minimally required security controls (for AFIN connection) or configurations.

2.22.2. Air Force Risk Management Council (AFRMC). The AFRMC provides a forum for the senior cybersecurity professionals to discuss issues concerning cybersecurity risk from a mission and business perspective. The council reviews proposed Mission Area or AF RMF control overlays, and RMF guidance. The council standardizes the cybersecurity implementation processes for both the acquisition and lifecycle operations for IT. The AFRMC advises and makes recommendations to existing governance bodies. Finally, the AFRMC recommends assignment of IT to the appropriate AO for systems that fall outside of all defined authorization boundaries.

2.22.3. AF AO Summit. The AO Summit is not a governance body but rather an enabler for both an enterprise-wide and converged organizational perspective to cybersecurity policy development, oversight, implementation, and training. This venue provides the SAF/CIO A6 and AOs an opportunity to discuss issues relevant to the RMF, AO Boundaries, IT, AOs, and SCAs.

2.22.4. For additional information on these forums, please see the SAF/CIO A6Z Cybersecurity Division site, AFI 17-130, applicable charters, and process guides.

Chapter 3

RMF METHODOLOGY

3.1. Overview.

3.1.1. The 6-Step RMF process at RMF Tier 3 (system level) is based on the process outlined in NIST SP 800-37r1 and DoDI 8510.01 and is illustrated in Figure 3.1. Where possible, this Instruction also identifies steps required for the "Assess Only" process. This process is iterative throughout the entire lifecycle for IT IAW DoDI 5000.02 and the *DoD Program Manager's Guidebook for Integrating the Cybersecurity Risk Management Framework (RMF) into the System Acquisition Lifecycle* (DoD PM Guidebook).

3.1.2. The DoD RMF KS is the authoritative source for RMF implementation, planning, and execution.

3.1.3. This chapter highlights the AF-specific implementation, key AF roles in each step, and additional resources required to complete the process. This Instruction is intended to be a companion to the DoD implementation instructions. Specific implementation guidance is available on the DoD RMF KS. Additionally, supplementary guidance concerning the execution of RMF steps for discrete classes of AF systems (e.g., financial systems) is contained in the Attachments.

Figure 3.1. RMF for AF IT.

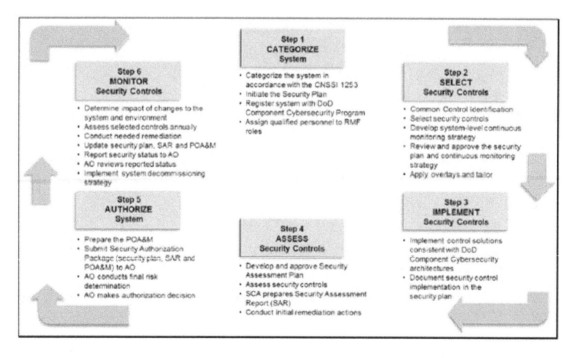

3.2. RMF Step 1, CATEGORIZE System. References DoDI 8510.01, CNSSI No.1253, NIST SP 800-53r4, NIST SP 800-60, *Guide for Mapping Types of Information and Information Systems to Security Categories,* and the DoD RMF KS.

3.2.1. Begin this step by completing the RMF IT Categorization and Selection Checklist and DD Form 2930, Privacy Impact Assessment. During categorization, the impact to confidentiality, integrity, and accessibility is categorized into one of three designations (low, moderate, or high) to address the impact of a loss. If the program's primary mission is not represented on the form's Authorization Boundary list, the PM or ISO will check "other" on the IT Categorization Checklist and submit the completed document to the AFRMC for disposition; send to SAF/CIO A6ZC Cybersecurity Division, **usaf.pentagon.saf-cio-a6.mbx.a6sc-workflow@mail.mil**. SAF/CIO A6ZC retains the IT categorized as "other" until the new AO Authorization Boundary is created or an AO is assigned. If an existing boundary is determined, the Checklist is returned to the PM/ISO for staffing to and approval by the determined AOs.

3.2.2. Each AF IT, IAW AFI 17-110, must be registered in EITDR, as the governance tool for the AF CIO, with the exception of those identified by other policy (i.e., space, Nuclear Command, Control, and Communication (NC3), Joint) to be registered in another repository. **(T-1)** EITDR/ITIPS will systematically assign a temporary registration number for each registered IT until the next scheduled replication with DoD Information Technology Portfolio Repository (DITPR). A DITPR number will then be systematically assigned and included in EITDR/ITIPS as the permanent official IT registration number for all registered AF IT.

NOTE: The EITDR system is transitioning to ITIPS by the end of 2nd quarter of 2017. When this system, or any future tracking system, is implemented, the EITDR registration requirements still apply in the current tracking system. All instances within this Instruction that reference EITDR is equivalent to ITIPS; consider these names interchangeable.

3.2.3. PMs or ISOs deploying systems across DoD/AF Components will register the system and post the categorization checklist to Enterprise Mission Assurance Support Service (eMASS).

3.2.4. For programs where the sensitivity of information may present a cybersecurity concern, the program (e.g., Aircraft, C2, and Weapons Systems) is required to upload only the following information/documentation into eMASS: PM and System Information eMASS fields, IT Categorization and Selection Checklist document, Cybersecurity Strategy document, Authorization Decision Memo document, and a Statement in the POA&M comments section (eMASS field) indicating the number of POA&M entries for the system. All documentation will be regularly reviewed to ensure accuracy and completeness, which may be audited by SAF/CIO A6ZC, Cybersecurity, the AO, or the SCA at any time.

3.2.5. Register all IT in the appropriate eMASS instance: NIPRNet eMASS or SIPRNet eMASS. Both instances have the same capabilities. Please note, SIPRNet eMASS is not certified to store TOP SECRET, SCI, or SAP/SAR artifacts or implementation details. NIPRNet eMASS is not certified to store SECRET artifacts or implementation details. The assigned SCA protects artifacts with special handling requirements. In those cases, the implementation plan or test results should simply state a 0 level (Compliant or Non-Compliant) and a reference to where the associated artifacts can be located.

3.2.6. The organization's eMASS Account Manager grants access to eMASS and grants required permissions based on duties and responsibilities. A listing of Account Managers for the AF organizations can be found on the SAF/CIO A6ZC Cybersecurity eMASS site.

3.3. RMF Step 2, SELECT Security Controls. References DoDI 8510.01, CNSSI No.1253, NIST SP 800-30, NIST SP 800-53r4, and the DoD's RMF KS.

3.3.1. The process for selection of security controls is: common control identification; security control baseline and overlay selection; tailoring (modification); ISCM strategy; and security plan and ISCM strategy review and approval.

3.3.2. Common Control Identification (available via eMASS).

3.3.2.1. DoD/AF Tier I/II Inheritance model: Common Controls (Policy).

3.3.2.2. AFSPC, the Enterprise AO and Common Control Provider, provides the Tier II Common Controls (Inheritance) available in eMASS for AF IT use.

3.3.2.3. Air Force Network NIPRNet RMF Inheritance – Core Services; this AFNET RMF package provides inheritance for AFNET Core Services for NIPRNet systems.

3.3.2.4. Air Force Network NIPRNet RMF Inheritance – Security; this AFNET RMF package provides inheritance for AFNET Security for NIPRNet systems.

3.3.2.5. Air Force Network NIPRNet RMF Inheritance – Transport; this AFNET RMF package provides inheritance for AFNET Transport Services for NIPRNet systems.

3.3.2.6. Air Force Network NIPRNet RMF Inheritance – Circuit Enclave (combined); this AFNET RMF package provides security, transport, and core inheritance for AFNET systems.

3.3.2.7. Air Force Network SIPRNet RMF Inheritance – Circuit Enclave (combined); this AFNET-S RMF package provides security, transport, and core inheritance for AFNET-S systems.

3.3.3. The security control baseline is selected based on the IT categorization.

3.3.4. Identify and apply overlays that apply to the AF IT. See **Chapter 5**.

3.3.5. Tailor controls as required. Every selected control must be accounted for either by the organization or the ISO. If a control is added or de-selected from the baseline (i.e., tagged as not applicable), then a risk-based rationale must be documented in the security plan and POA&M. Also, if a selected control will not be implemented, document a risk-informed rationale (i.e., using a cost/benefit analysis) for not planning to implement the control must be documented in the security plan and POA&M.

3.3.6. Operational Technology (OT) is more sensitive to the application of cyber security measures and controls that can affect its availability. Many forms of OT are categorized as types of PIT systems, PIT subsystems, or PIT products. An AO with OT within their authorization boundary is responsible for managing the risk for OT and may tailor controls to balance security and availability.

3.3.7. ISCM strategy. Develop and document a system-level ISCM strategy for the continuous monitoring of the effectiveness of security controls employed within or inherited by the system, and monitoring of any proposed or actual changes to the system and its environment of operation.

3.3.8. ISCM Capabilities. CTOs were issued to implement Host Based Security System (HBSS) and Assured Compliance Assessment Solution (ACAS) tools in support of continuous monitoring.

3.3.9. ISCM strategy review and approval. The AO's staff will develop and implement processes whereby the AO (or designee) reviews and approves the security plan and ISCM strategy submitted by the PM or ISO.

3.4. RMF Step 3, IMPLEMENT Security Controls. References DoDI 8510.01, NIST SP 800-53r4, applicable Security Technical Implementation Guides (STIG), Security Requirements Guides (SRG), and the DoD's RMF KS. (STIGs and SRGs can be found on the DISA website).

3.4.1. Enterprise Architecture, IAW AFI 17-100, *Air Force Information Technology (IT) Service Management*, the Target, Implementation, and Operational Baselines (TB, IB, and OB) address the technical standards, protocols and guidance to establish a consistent environment for IT capability engineering, development, deployment and support. The Baselines are prescriptive and include the items required for a repeatable process to develop and deploy IT capabilities.

3.4.2. Place Contract Data Requirements List (CDRL) items for architecture, design, integration, and verification artifacts on contract to receive the implementation detail for security controls to support risk assessment. Document the implementation in the security plan.

3.5. RMF Step 4, ASSESS Security Controls. References DoDI 8510.01, NIST SP 800-30, NIST 800-53Ar4, applicable STIGs, SRGs, and the DoD's RMF KS. Use DoDI 8510.01, enclosure 6 instructions for details for assessing security controls.

3.6. RMF Step 5, AUTHORIZE System. After reviewing the security authorization documentation, the AO formally accepts or rejects risk by authorizing the IT through an IATT, ATO, ATO with conditions, or a DATO. References DoDI 8510.01, enclosure 6.

3.6.1. AOs may issue an IATT, ATO, or an ATO with conditions for any risk determined not to be "Very High" or "High". **(T-0)**

3.6.2. ATO with conditions for unmitigated "Very High" or "High" risk.

3.6.2.1. The SAF/CIO A6 is the only Air Force member who may grant IT to operate (receive an ATO with conditions) with "Very High" or "High" risk (formerly known as CAT I) non-compliant security controls that cannot be corrected or mitigated immediately, but where the overall risk is acceptable. Delegation below the AF CIO is not authorized. IT with "Very High" or "High" risk, which are authorized by other DoD Components connecting to the AFIN require their Component CIO approval, and joint systems require DoD CIO approval.

3.6.2.2. IT with unmitigated "Very High" or "High" risk non-compliant security controls must follow the Very High/High Package Submission Guide and submit completed packages to the SAF/CIO A6 for approval prior to making an authorization decision. **(T-0)**

3.6.2.3. For "Very High" or "High" risk authorizations, the ATO with conditions can be issued for up to 1 year. When a 1-year ATO with conditions is issued, the ATO with conditions specifies a review period that is within 6 months of the authorization termination date (ATD). **(T-1)**

3.6.2.4. If the system still requires operation with a level of risk of "Very High" or "High" after 1 year, the AF CIO must again grant permission for continued operation of the system. **(T-0)**

3.7. Denial of Authorization to Operate (DATO).

3.7.1. If risk is determined to be unacceptable when compared to the mission assurance requirement, then the AO, in collaboration with all program stakeholders, will issue the authorization decision in the form of a DATO. If the system is already operational, the responsible AO will issue a DATO and operation of the system will cease immediately. Network connections will be immediately terminated for any system that is issued a DATO.

3.7.2. Upon issuing the DATO, the AO will provide a copy of the issued document to SAF/CIO A6 via **usaf.pentagon.saf-cio-a6.mbx.a6sc-workflow@mail.mil**.

3.8. RMF Step 6, MONITOR Security Controls. References DoDI 8510.01 and NIST SP 800-137, *Information Security Continuous Monitoring (ISCM)*.

3.8.1. DoDI 8510.01 and the DoD RMF KS for Continuous Monitoring provides a detailed framework on continuous monitoring, which should be used to augment the continuous monitoring program for the IT.

3.8.2. If a system-level ISCM strategy is not yet developed or executed, as a minimum, periodically assess a subset of the selected controls using a team (e.g., ISSM, sys admin, CSSP, PM, ISO) to ensure any changes are immediately addressed the impact to the system, mission, and capabilities are determined. The periodic assessment is documented in the security assessment report (SAR). The PM updates the POA&M and security plan documents with the new vulnerabilities.

3.8.3. Following the issuance of the authorization decision and establishment of a security baseline (i.e., ATO or ATO with conditions), any changes to the system must be assessed by the system's ISSM to ascertain if the change has a security impact. The ISSM is critical in the initiation of the change review process. The ISSM must consult the SCA for an assessment of any change to the system to determine if re-authorization is required. The rule of thumb is that if the implementation of a security control is affected by the change (especially for IA or IA-enabled products), there must be a validation of the security control implementation, as in the initial assessment effort. Therefore, the authorization is at jeopardy, and the SCA must assess the implementation and assessment of the security control/s and determine if the risk level remains consistent with the current authorization.

3.8.4. If the ISSM determines the system change does not adversely affect the security baseline of the system (i.e., no security impact (NSI)), the system may continue to operate under its current authorization decision. Changes are documented and included with the system security documentation and RMF documentation. The ISSM must provide a synopsis of the NSI to the SCA for concurrence. If the SCA concurs with the NSI, a new authorization decision and connection approval is not required.

3.8.5. If the ISSM determines a change impacts the security baseline of the system, the SCA must evaluate the change and determine the appropriate course of action; that is, the SCA could direct use of an independent validator (i.e., an ASCA) for hands-on evaluation of the system. If the SCA concurs the change impacts the security baseline of the system, and/or a weakness cannot be mitigated in a timely manner to bring the risk back to the level the AO accepted in the current authorization, a new authorization decision and connection approval is required. NOTE: If the change results in a new "Very High" or "High" risk non-compliant security control(s) that can be corrected within 30 days or a new Moderate risk that can be corrected/satisfactorily mitigated within 90 days, the system can continue to operate under the existing authorization decision and connection approval as referenced in DoDI 8510.01.

3.9. Resources and Tools.

3.9.1. DoD PM Guidebook. The *DoD Program Manager's Guidebook for Integrating the Cybersecurity Risk Management Framework (RMF) into the System Acquisition Lifecycle*, The DoD PM Guidebook supports the policies in this AFI by providing specific procedures and is capable of implementing changes as industry and policy dictate. **(T-0)**

3.9.2. PIT Cybersecurity Guidebook. *The Platform Information Technology (PIT) Cybersecurity Guidebook* provides clarity on the information cybersecurity activities required for all PIT. This includes weapon systems, medical systems, industrial control systems, armament systems, test systems, etc., that qualify as PIT. The Guidebook should be used to develop local procedures, as enhancement to RMF for PIT that correspond with the product being developed or procured. The Guidebook suggests best practices to be followed in ensuring cybersecurity is "built-in" to the product, but allows local variations. The primary use of the Guidebook is for acquisition of new PIT and to provide guidance on applicability of the RMF to legacy PIT.

3.9.3. ASCA Licensing Guide. The number and complexity of AF IT may require the AF SCA to designate qualified entities as ASCA to perform assessment actions. The AF SCA created the ASCA *Licensing Guide* to appoint licensed, qualified agents to provide accurate, consistent, and trusted AF and Space IT assessments.

3.9.4. Plan of Actions and Milestones (POA&M).

3.9.4.1. The IT security POA&M is a tool that identifies tasks that need to be accomplished to mitigate systems weaknesses and reduce risk. It details resources required to accomplish the elements of the plan, any milestones in meeting the task, and scheduled completion dates for the milestones. The purpose of the POA&M is to assist agencies in identifying, assessing, prioritizing, and monitoring the progress of corrective efforts for security weaknesses found in IT. For further POA&M information, refer to the Air Force POA&M Guidebook.

3.9.4.2. SAF/CIO A6ZC will monitor and track the overall execution of system-level IT security POA&Ms (on behalf of the AF CIO and CISO) until identified security weaknesses are closed and the RMF documentation appropriately adjusted. **(T-0)**

3.9.4.3. The PM or ISO is responsible for implementing the corrective actions identified in the IT security POA&M and, with the support and assistance of the ISSM, will provide visibility and status to the ISO, AO, and the AF CIO. **(T-0)**

Chapter 4

APPROVAL TO CONNECT (ATC) PROCESS

4.1. Overview. The ATC process is one instance of the AF's implementation of reciprocity between AOs. It is a formal evaluation of the risk of connecting systems to the receiving enclave; the ATC is a means to manage community risk. Having an ATO does not entitle systems to an ATC from the receiving AO.

NOTE: Although this Instruction specifies the requirements for connections to the AFIN, other AOs are encouraged to utilize this process to authorize connections to enclaves within their authorization (formerly accreditation) boundary.

4.2. Duration and Expiration. In order for a system to request an ATC from a site or enclave, both the AF system and the destination enclave must have a valid and current authorization. The system ATC expiration date will be no later than the ATD of the ATO for that system. For a system under continual reauthorization, the connection authorization must be reevaluated upon a significant system modification, significant change to the threat or risk posture, or every 3 years, whichever comes first.

4.3. Connection to the DoDIN. For enclaves requiring a circuit connection from DISA, ISSMs must follow the DISN Connection Process Guide to ensure all required artifacts are provided on initial submission. Connection requests will be coordinated through the AF Enterprise AO.

4.4. Connection to the Air Force Information Networks (AFIN). The AF Enterprise AO is the only authority permitted to grant an ATC to the AFIN. The Enterprise AO may delegate this authority to appropriate representatives with concurrence of the SAF/CIO A6.

4.4.1. AF systems authorized through the AF Enterprise AO will receive an ATC after the system is reviewed for compliance with the required security controls and the community risk imposed by the connecting system is determined to be at an acceptable level.

4.4.2. AF systems authorized through another AF AO will submit the ATC request through eMASS.

4.4.3. Non-AF owned systems with approved authorizations (i.e., "Guest System", see para 4.5) are required to have an ATC request initiated in eMASS by the AF sponsor, the PM, or ISO before the IT connects to the AFIN.

4.4.4. The AF Enterprise SCA will identify and maintain a listing of the Tier I/II (common) security controls on the RMF KS, Air Force Component Workspace. Furthermore, the AF Enterprise SCA will specify continuous monitoring requirements for each of the identified common controls. **(T-0)**

4.4.5. Certain security controls are designated as required (to address community risk concerns) of all systems requesting a connection to the AFIN. Some of these required controls may be inherited from the Tier 1/II Common security controls. Required controls may not be tailored out during the security control selection or tailoring steps. Regardless of the source (i.e., Tier I/II inherited or provide by the system), a status of "Compliant" or "Non-Compliant" is required for each of these controls. The assessment of these controls and associated artifacts will determine whether the AF system poses an unacceptable risk to the AFIN or other systems connected to or residing on the AFIN (i.e., imposes community risk). Furthermore, the AF Enterprise SCA will specify continuous monitoring requirements for each of the identified required controls.

4.4.6. The AF Enterprise AO will document the ATC decision in eMASS. **(T-1)**

4.5. Guest System Registration. A special case, limited registration of a system that is authorized by a non-AF Authorizing Official, or is owned by a non-Air Force organization but is hosted within the AFIN.

4.5.1. IT identified as a Guest System must the name of the AF sponsor to **usaf.pentagon.saf-cio-a6.mbx.a6sc-workflow@mail.mil.**

4.5.2. Provide the following information in your request: System acronym, system name, brief system description, ATD, and organization that granted the authorization. If possible, identify the AF community which will use the system and a recommended sponsor.

4.5.3. The appointed sponsor is documented in a sponsorship memo prepared by SAF/CIO A6. The AF sponsor will then enter the system into eMASS and act as a liaison with the external customer. Systems authorized by another AO are required, as a minimum, to provide a topology and valid authorization for the system being connected. Additionally, the following RMF artifacts or other equivalent are required: Sponsor memo; authorization decision; port, protocol, and services (PPS) listing; hardware/software list; SAR; and POA&M. Additionally, space systems identified as AF IT investments must register in EITDR/ITIPS. **(T-1)**

4.6. ATC Process for Air Force Functional/Mission Systems.

4.6.1. AF functional/mission systems (e.g., A4, SAF/FM, PMOs) systems with an AF Authorization to Operate (ATO), Interim Authorization to Test (IATT), or Authorization to Operate (ATO) with conditions signed by an AF AO (other than the AF Enterprise AO) require an ATC to the AFIN.

4.6.2. The Functional/Mission System PM or AO Staff is responsible for submitting requests for obtaining an ATC from the AF Enterprise AO. For systems/enclaves connecting to/through the AFIN, ATC requests are submitted to the AF Enterprise AO in eMASS as a "Guest System". For systems/enclaves connecting to/through the AFNET or AFNET-S, ATC requests are submitted to the AF Enterprise AO through "Manage ATC" function in eMASS. Contact the AF Enterprise AO staff for other connection (contractor, commercial Internet service provider, direct) AO's POC for information and guidance.

4.7. Continuous Monitoring. AF IT ISSMs must ensure the controls identified as required for an ATC are monitored IAW the published continuous monitoring strategy guidance. The details will be included in the system-level ISCM strategy and evaluated and approved by the receiving AO. **(T-0)** If the system fails to meet the continuous monitoring requirements, a Denial of Approval to Connect (DATC) may be issued.

4.8. Denial of Approval to Connect (DATC). A DATC may be issued for any IT (connected to the AFIN or other AF enclave) at any time, if the AO determines the risk to the receiving enclave is too high. The PM or ISO is notified immediately of the DATC.

4.8.1. If the system is already connected, the connection must be terminated upon signature of the DATC.

4.8.2. All denial decisions must be signed by the hosting enclave AO, and cannot be delegated further.

Chapter 5

SECURITY CONTROL OVERLAYS

5.1. Overview. Overlays provide communities of interest an opportunity for consistent tailoring of security controls based on risk specific to a type of information, system, or environment. They include characteristics and assumptions about the overlay topic, security control and control enhancement specifications, risk-based rationale for control specifications (tied back to the characteristics/assumptions) supplemental guidance, and tailoring guidance designed to refine the control selection and tailoring process.

5.2. Policy. The DoD may vet all AF overlays for consideration as a DoD or CNSS overlay. The cognizant authorities over the type of information, system, or environment that is the subject of the overlay and who are principally impacted by the use of a proposed overlay will (with the support and concurrence of all affected parties) generate and approve overlays. The AF CISO will approve overlays that have AF-wide impact.

5.3. Development and Approval Process. Follow the process outlined in the AF Approved Overlay Process to develop and approve overlays for use on AF IT.

5.3.1. Send topic to AF Cybersecurity TAG Chairs. (OPR: Overlay Proposer) All potential topics for overlays are submitted to the AF Cybersecurity TAG Chairs for validation. Topics should be sent to **usaf.pentagon.saf-cio-a6.mbx.a6sc-workflow@mail.mil**. The topics should include the following information: Name of proposed overlay; use case for overlay application; summary of the unique characteristics that drive the need to tailor controls; applicable laws, regulations, or directives governing the application of the overlay; and point of contact information.

5.3.2. Validate Topic. (OPR: AF Cybersecurity TAG) The TAG Chairs will provide the proposed overlay information to TAG members for an electronic vote. The TAG will consider whether the proposed overlay is relevant to AF IT, as well as ensure there are no conflicts with overlays in development, approved, or disapproved previously. Adjustments to the topic may be made in coordination with the overlay proposer.

5.3.3. Follow AF Overlay Development and Approval Process. (OPR: Overlay Proposer) If approved, the Overlay Development Team will follow the approved AF Overlay Development and Approval Process. The overlay development team should coordinate with SAF/CIO A6ZC, Cybersecurity Division, throughout the development process.

5.3.4. Support Overlay Development. (OPR: Overlay Proposer/ Overlay Development Team; OCR: SAF/CIO A6, Cybersecurity) The Overlay Proposer is responsible for identifying an Overlay Development Team to build the overlay and supporting documentation. SAF/CIO A6ZC, Cybersecurity Division, can assist with the policy requirements for the overlay.

5.3.5. Develop Overlay. (OPR: Overlay Proposer, Overlay Development Team, OCR: ISSM, AF CISO) Use the template provided in CNSSI No. 1253, Appendix F, Attachment 2 to develop the overlay. In addition to the specified controls, the Overlay Development Team must include any adjustments to implementation guidance, assessment procedures, and specific assignment values for the selected controls. The tailoring guidance must clearly state any limitations or restrictions to guide application of the overlay. All security control specifications must be justified based on the risk specific to the type of information, system, or environment that is the topic of the overlay, and that risk must trace back to a characteristic and/or assumption clearly stated in the front matter of the overlay.

5.4. Review and Coordinate Finalized Overlay.

5.4.1. **(OPR: SAF/CIO A6ZC, Cybersecurity Division)** When the Overlay Development Team is completed required actions, the overlay and overlay approval memorandum is provided to SAF/CIO A6ZC for review and posting, as applicable (mission system use, AF or other use, and dissemination). SAF/CIO A6ZC will review the selected controls, implementation guidance, assessment procedures, specific assignment values, and tailoring guidance for compliance with the CNSSI No. 1253 format. If there are discrepancies in the overlay, the submitting organization must address those prior to gaining final approval.

5.4.2. **(OPR: Overlay proposer)** Overlays are developed to address risks specific to the type of information, system, or environment; therefore, as the risk changes so should the overlay. Ensure review and modification of the overlay are captured in the security plan and other applicable documentation.

5.5. Coordinate with DISA to Implement Overlay in eMASS. (OPR: SAF/CIO A6, Cybersecurity) SAF/CIO A6ZC, Cybersecurity Division, will coordinate with DISA to implement the approved overlay in the NIPRNet and SIPRNet instances of eMASS. Restrictions on use approved by the Mission Area Owner will be communicated to DISA.

Chapter 6

TRANSFER OF IT BETWEEN AUTHORIZING OFFICIALS

6.1. Overview. Every IT system must be properly aligned to an AO. **(T-1)** The overall objective is to ensure the transition process is standard and consistent. The transition process is defined as the transfer of IT to include documentation from one AO to another AO. It is a collaborative process executed by the owning AO and coordinated with the receiving AO. The Request Transfer of Information Technology to Another Authorizing Official form (available on the AF RMF KS) will be used to facilitate an orderly and timely transfer of IT. Transferring IT, projected transfer dates, and system transfer preconditions will be coordinated with the applicable AOs and their staffs. The AOs will ensure process accountability and situational/stakeholder awareness throughout this process.

6.2. Transition Process. The transition process steps are as follows:

6.2.1. The owning AO staff, in coordination with the PM or ISO, if no PM is assigned, identifies the IT to transfer from an owning AO to the receiving AO.

6.2.2. As the AO staff identifies IT for transfer, it is important to include the MAJCOM Portfolio Manager (PfM) of the IT in this identification process, as the PfM has an integral role in all IT transfer actions.

6.2.3. The owning AO reviews and approves the proposed IT to transfer to the receiving AO.

6.2.4. The PM or ISO of the IT completes the Request Transfer of Information Technology to Another Authorizing Official Form for each IT.

6.2.5. The owning AO staff, in coordination with the PM/ISO and PfM, contacts the receiving AO staff/PM to discuss the proposed IT transfer.

6.2.6. The receiving AO staff completes the Assessment/Notes section of Request Transfer of Information Technology to Another Authorizing Official Form.

6.2.7. The owning AO and receiving AO agree to the transfer (skip to 6.2.9).

6.2.8. If the receiving AO disagrees with the transfer, the owning AO staff will request assistance from the AFRMC by sending the Request Transfer of Information Technology to Another Authorizing Official Form to SAF-CIO A6ZC workflow at **usaf.pentagon.saf-cio-a6.mbx.a6sc-workflow@mail.mil**. The AFRMC will adjudicate the inclusion/transfer of the IT and provide a recommendation to the CISO as the final decision authority.

6.2.9. Once the IT transfer is agreed to by both AOs, the owning AO and receiving AO sign the Request Transfer of Information Technology to Another Authorizing Official Form.

6.2.10. The PM/ISO, in coordination with the PfM, will make required changes in EITDR/ITIPS and eMASS.

6.3. IT With No AO Assigned. Systems not currently under any AO's authority, not fitting into an authorization boundary, or not accepted by the gaining AO are addressed by the AFRMC. If the IT Categorization and Selection Checklist identifies the IT should be assigned in the "other" AO Authorization Boundary, then SAF/CIO A6ZC, Cybersecurity Division, retains the IT until the new AO Authorization Boundary is created and an AO is assigned. If an existing boundary is determined, the submitted IT Categorization and Selection Checklist is returned to the PM/ISO for staffing to and approval by the determined AO.

Chapter 7

RMF TRANSITION

7.1. Overview. All IT will transition to the RMF IAW DoDI 8510.01. In addition, the PM or ISO will ensure all IT is in compliance with the timelines specified below. These timelines provide the latest date a DIACAP package may be submitted for C&A and provide RMF submission guidance. The RMF timeline does not prevent a PM or ISO from moving to the RMF sooner than the times specified below. New and existing systems utilizing a contract shall include contract language ensuring the IT complies with the RMF, which may require modification to the contract language. Acquisition requirement officials shall ensure new requirements/systems are compliant with this Instruction and existing systems must be modified to utilize the RMF by the dates below.

7.2. Transition Timeline.

7.2.1. AOs will establish transition timelines for all AF IT (new and existing) within their purview.

7.2.2. PMs or ISOs may submit completed DIACAP packages to the AO for signature until 1 March 2017 (AF specific deadline), and the ATD is determined by the AO signature date, but no DIACAP authorization may exceed 31 March 2018 without an approved RMF Deviation Request.

7.2.3. All packages submitted after 1 March 2017 (AF specific deadline) must comply with RMF policy and guidance (i.e., be in the format of the RMF security authorization package).

7.3. RMF Deviation Requests.

7.3.1. In the case of a significant financial or operational impact due to transitioning to the RMF, an AO may submit a request for deviation to the SAF/CIO A6 for approval.

7.3.2. Requests for deviation must include an RMF transition plan and a POA&M.

7.3.3. Requests are submitted to SAF/CIO A6ZC Cybersecurity, usaf.pentagon.saf-cio-a6.mbx.a6sc-workflow@mail.mil, for coordination by the CISO and approval by the SAF/CIO A6.

7.3.4. An approved deviation request does not relieve the IT from maintaining an acceptable risk posture.

WILLIAM J. BENDER, Lt Gen, USAF
Chief of Information Dominance and
Chief Information Officer

Attachment 1

GLOSSARY OF REFERENCES AND SUPPORTING INFORMATION

References

AFI 10-1701, *Command and Control (C2) for Cyberspace Operations*, March 5, 2014

AFI 16-701, *Management, Administration and Oversite of Special Access Programs,* 18 February, 2014

AFI 33-115, *Air Force Information Technology (IT) Service Management*, September 16, 2014

AFI 33-141, *Air Force Information Technology Portfolio Management and IT Investment Review*, December 23, 2008

AFI 17-130, *Air Force Cybersecurity Program Management*

AFI 33-360, *Publications and Forms Management*, December 1, 2015

AFI 33-401, *Air Force Architecting*, May 17, 2011

AFI 63-101/20-101, *Integrated Life Cycle Management,* March 7, 2013

AFMAN 33-153, *Information Technology (IT) Asset Management (ITAM),* March 19, 2014

AFMAN 17-1303, *Cybersecurity Workforce Improvement Program*

AFMAN 33-363, *Management of Records*, March 1, 2008

AFMAN 33-407, *Air Force Clinger-Cohen Act (CCA) Compliance Guide*, October 24, 2012

AFPD 17-1, *Information Dominance Governance and Management,* 12 April 2016

AFPD 33-3, *Information Management*, September 8, 2011

CJCSI 6211.02D, *Defense Information System Network (DISN) Responsibilities,* January 24, 2012

CJCSI 6510.01F, *Information Assurance (IA) and Support to Computer Network Defense (CND)*, February 9, 2011

CNSSI No. 1253, *Security Categorization and Control Selection for National Security Systems*, March 27, 2014

CNSSI No. 4009, *Committee on National Security Systems (CNSS) Glossary*, April 6, 2015

CNSSI No. 4016, *National Information Assurance Training Standard for Risk Analysis,* November 2005.

CNSSP No. 11, *National Policy Governing the Acquisition of Information Assurance* (IA) *and IA-Enabled Information Technology Products*, June 10, 2013

Defense Federal Acquisition Regulation Supplement (DFARS) clause 252.204-7012, October 2016

DoD Comptroller, *Financial Improvement and Audit Readiness* (FIAR) *Guidance*, April 2015

DoD Program Manager's Guidebook for Integrating the Cybersecurity Risk Management Framework (RMF) into the System Acquisition Lifecycle v1.1, September 2015

DoDD 8000.01, *Management of the Department of Defense Information Enterprise (DoD IE)*, March 16, 2016

DoDI 5000.02, *Operation of the Defense Acquisition System*, January 7, 2015

DoDI 5200.02, *DoD Personnel Security Program (PSP)*, March 21, 2014

DoDI 5200.08, *Security of DoD Installations and resources and the DoD Physical Security Review Board (PSRB)*, December 10, 2005

DoDI 5205.13, *Defense Industrial Base* (DIB) *Cybersecurity/ Information Assurance* (CS/IA) *Activities*, January 29, 2010

DoDI 8500.01, *Cybersecurity*, March 14, 2014

DoDI 8510.01, *Risk Management Framework (RMF) for DoD Information Technology (IT)*, March 12, 2014

DoDI 8551.01, *Ports, Protocols, and Services Management (PPSM)*, May 28, 2014

DoDI 8580.1, *Information Assurance in the Defense Acquisition System*, July 9, 2004

DoDM 5200.01, Volume 1, *DoD Information Security Program: Overview, Classification, and Declassification*, February 24, 2012

DoDM 5200.01, Volume 2, *DoD Information Security Program: Marking of Classified Information*, February 24, 2012

DoDM 5200.01, Volume 3, *DoD Information Security Program: Protection of Classified Information*, February 24, 2012

DoDM 5200.01, Volume 4, *DoD Information Security Program: Controlled Unclassified Information (CUI)*, February 24, 2012

Federal Information Security Modernization Act of 2014

GAO-09-232G, *Federal Information System Controls Audit Manual* (FISCAM), February 2009

Joint Publication (JP) 1-02, *Department of Defense Dictionary of Military and Associated Terms*, January 15, 2016

NIST SP 800-137, *Information Security Continuous Monitoring (ISCM) for Federal Information Systems and Organizations,* September 2011

NIST SP 800-171, *Protecting Controlled Unclassified Information in Nonfederal Information Systems and Organizations,* June 2015

NIST SP 800-18, *Guide for Developing Security Plans for Federal Information Systems*, February 2006

NIST SP 800-30, *Guide for Conducting Risk Assessments*, September 2012

NIST SP 800-37r1, *Guide for Applying the Risk Management Framework to Federal Information Systems: A Security Life Cycle Approach*, February 2010

NIST SP 800-53A, *Assessing Security and Privacy Controls in Federal Information Systems and Organizations*, Dec 2014.

NIST SP 800-53r4, *Security and Privacy Controls for Federal Information Systems and Organizations*, April 2013

NIST SP 800-60, *Volume 1: Guide for Mapping Types of Information and Information Systems to Security Categories*, August 2008

NIST SP 800-60, *Volume 2: Appendices to Guide for Mapping Types of Information and Information Systems to Security Categories*, August 2008

NIST SP 800-82, *Guide to Industrial Control Systems (ICS) Security: Supervisory Control and Data Acquisition (SCADA) Systems, Distributed Control Systems (DCS), and Other Control System Configurations such as Programmable Logic Controllers (PLC)*, May 2015

OMB Circular A-123 as revised, *Management's Responsibility for Internal Control*, 21 December 2004

OMB Circular A-130, *Managing Information as a Strategic Resource,* July 28, 2016

Title 10 USC § 2224, *Defense Information Assurance Program*, January 7, 2011

Title 44 USC § 3541, *Information Security*

Title 44 USC § 3602, *Office of Electronic Government*, December 17, 2002

Title 5 United States Code (USC) § 552a, *The Privacy Act of 1974, as amended* January 7, 2011

Abbreviations and Acronyms

AF—Air Force

AFCTA—Air Force Cybersecurity Technical Advisory Group

AF EPL—AF Evaluated Products List

AF SACA—Air Force Software and Application Certification Assessment

AFI—Air Force Instruction

AFIN—Air Force Information Networks

AFMAN—Air Force Manual

AFNET—Air Force Network - The AF's underlying Non-Secure Internet Protocol Router Net (NIPRNet)

AFNET-S—Air Force Network – SECRET - The Air Force's underlying Secure Internet Protocol Router Network (SIPRNet)

AFNIC—Air Force Network Integration Center

AFPD—Air Force Policy Directive

AFRIMS—Air Force Records Information Management System

AFRMC—Air Force Risk Management Council

AFSPC—Air Force Space Command

AO—Authorizing Official

AODR—Authorizing Official Designated Representative

ARW—Application Request Worksheet

BMA—Business Mission Area

C2—Command and Control

CAL—Category Assurance List

CIO—Chief Information Officer

CJCSI—Chairman of the Joint Chiefs of Staff Instruction

CND—Computer Network Defense

CNSSI—Committee on National Security Systems Instruction

CNSSP—Committee on National Security Systems Policy

COCOM—Combatant Command

COMSEC—Communications Security

COTS—Commercial Off-The-Shelf

CTO—Cyber Tasking Order

DATC—Denial of Approval to Connect

DATO—Denial of Authorization to Operate

DSCC—DoD Server Core Configuration

DFARS—Defense Federal Acquisition Regulation Supplement

DIB—Defense Industrial Base

DIMA—DoD Portion of the Intelligence Mission Area

DISA—Defense Information Systems Agency

DNI—Director of National Intelligence

DoD—Department of Defense

DoDD—Department of Defense Directive

DoDI—Department of Defense Instruction

DoDIN—Department of Defense Information Network

DSAWG—Defense Information Assurance Security Accreditation Working Group

EITDR—Enterprise Information Technology Data Repository

eMASS—Enterprise Mission Assurance Support Service

FAR—Federal Acquisition Regulation

FIPS—Federal Information Processing Standard

FISMA—Federal Information Security Modernization Act

HAF—Headquarters Air Force

HBSS—Host Based Security System

HQ AFSPC—Headquarters Air Force Space Command

IAW—In Accordance With

IC—Intelligence Community

ICD—Intelligence Community Directive

IEMA—Information Environment Mission Area

IP—Information Protection

IPO—Information Protection Office

IS—Information System

ISCM—Information Security Continuous Monitoring

ISSM—Information System Security Manager

ISSO—Information System Security Officer

ISO—Information System Owners

ISSE—Information System Security Engineering

ISSO—Information System Security Officer

IT—Information Technology

ITIPS—Information Technology Investment Portfolio System

JP—Joint Publication

MAO—Mission Area Owner

MAJCOM—Major Command

NC3—Nuclear Command Control and Communications

NIPRNet—Non-Secure Internet Protocol Router Network

NIST—National Institute of Standards and Technology

NSS—National Security System

OMB—Office of Management and Budget

OPR—Office of Primary Responsibility

OSS—Open Source Software

PII—Personally Identifiable Information

PIT—Platform Information Technology

PKI—Public Key Infrastructure

PM—Program Manager

PMO—Program Management Office

POA&M—Plan of Actions and Milestones

PPS—Ports, Protocol, and Services

PPSM—Ports, Protocol, and Services Management

RDS—Records Disposition Schedule

SAF—Secretary of the Air Force

SAP/SAR—Special-Access Program/Special Access Required

SCA—Security Control Assessor

SCI—Sensitive Compartmented Information

SDC—Standard Desktop Configuration

SECAF—Secretary of the Air Force

SIPRNet—Secret Internet Protocol Router Network

SP—Special Publication

SRG—Security Requirements Guides

STIG—Security Technical Implementation Guide

TAG—Technical Advisory Group

UR—User Representative

US—United States

USC—United States Code

USSTRATCOM—United States Strategic Command

WMA—Warfighting Mission Area

Terms

All terms used in this Instruction are defined in CNSSI No. 4009, DoDI 8500.01, or DoDI 8510.01, which may refer to authoritative NIST issuances. Any exceptions are defined below.

Agent of the Security Control Assessor—The licensed person or organization that acts as an independent trusted agent of the SCA, providing fact-based security analysis.

Approval to Connect—The official management decision given by a senior organizational official to authorize connection of an information system to an enclave and to explicitly accept the risk to organizational operations (including mission, functions, image, or reputation), organizational assets, individuals, other organizations, and the Nation based on the implementation of an agreed-upon set of security controls.

Guest System—A special case, limited registration of a system that is authorized by a non-AF Authorizing Official, or is owned by a non-Air Force organization but is hosted within the AFIN and must complete the process to acquire an approval to connect (ATC) from the AF Enterprise AO. A Guest System is a type of external information system (see CNSSI No. 4009).

Functional System—A system with a mission-unique function usually authorized by an AO other than the AF Enterprise AO (e.g., Global Command and Control System (GCCS), Global Decisions Support System (GDSS))

Operational Technology (OT)—IT adapted to directly monitor and control physical devices, processes, and events where availability is the primary operational concern.

PIT Subsystem—A collection of PIT that does not rise to the level of a PIT system.

PIT Product—Individual hardware or software components, including, but not limited to, operating systems, commercial or government software, or individual hardware that support specific mission functionality. IT Products, when purposed for PIT, become PIT Products.

Attachment 2

AF IT ASSESS ONLY REQUIREMENTS

1. PIT Subsystems, PIT Products, IT Services, and IT Products. IT categorized below the system level will not require an authorization decision. These IT will follow the Assess Only process. The IT below the system level must be securely configured (in accordance with applicable DoD policies and security controls), documented in an assessment package, and reviewed by the responsible ISSM, under the direction of the AO, for acceptance or connection into an authorized IS or PIT System.

1.1. PIT. The PIT system owner (i.e., ISO) may determine that a collection of PIT rises to the level of a PIT System with the AO's approval.

The ISSM (with the review and approval of the AO) is responsible for ensuring all PIT complete the appropriate RMF processes prior to incorporation into or connection to a system or enclave. PIT may be categorized using CNSSI No. 1253 with the resultant security control baselines tailored as needed. Otherwise, the specific cybersecurity needs of PIT must be assessed on a case-by-case basis and security controls applied as appropriate.

1.2. IT Services. Organizations that use internal IT services must ensure the categorization of the system delivering the service is appropriate to the confidentiality, integrity, and availability needs of the information and mission and that written agreements describing the roles and responsibilities of both the provider and the recipient are in place. Organizations that use external IT services provided by a non-DoD federal government agency, except cloud services, must ensure the categorization of the system delivering the service is appropriate to the confidentiality, integrity, and availability needs of the information and mission, and that the system delivering the service is operating under a current authorization from that agency. Organizations contracting for external IT services in the form of commercial cloud computing services must comply with DoD and AF cloud computing policy and procedural guidance.

1.3. IT Products. Products will be configured by the system administrator in accordance with applicable STIGs under a cognizant ISSM and SCA. STIGs are product specific and document applicable DoD policies and security requirements, as well as best practices and configuration guidelines. When a STIG is not available for a product, a Security Requirements Guide (SRG) may be used.

1.4. IT Product, Software, and Application Certification Assessment. ISSMs have the responsibility to exercise due diligence on IT product software and applications (software products) that reside on their enclave/system. At a minimum, software products will be assessed for supportability, operability, compatibility, and security to ensure the products present an acceptable risk to the AFIN. This can be accomplished via the following methods:

1.4.1. Assess and Authorize. ISSM's may incorporate software assessment and evaluation, giving the Software Assessment Report (SwAR) as part of their system enclave's security authorization package. Follow the guidance and use the template on the DoD RMF KS.

1.4.2. Air Force Software and Application Certification Assessment (AF SACA). Software products may be assessed through the AF SACA process managed by the Air Force Network Integration Center (AFNIC). The Enterprise SCA then certifies software products for inclusion on the AF Evaluated Products List (AF EPL). Testing may be accomplished by AFNIC or by the organization sponsoring the software product. Software products are certified for use on computers running the Standard Desktop Configuration or DoD Server Core Configuration, applications, and approved mobile devices on the AFIN. Instructions, templates, and the testing methodology are located on the <u>Software Certification Assessment home page</u>.

1.4.2.1. All assessments must be initiated and documented using an Application Request Worksheet (ARW). The ARW will be submitted and endorsed by the Wing ISSM or MAJCOM functional directorate.

1.4.2.2. Once the ARW is accepted by AFNIC, testing is accomplished by either the sponsor or AFNIC. The software assessment must be conducted on an environment external to the operational network.

1.4.2.3. If the software product presents an acceptable risk (e.g., low or very low) to the enclave, the major version of the product will be certified for up to 3 years by the AF Enterprise SCA and placed on the AF EPL. This certification is not an ATO. The system or enclave ISSM must implement any required mitigations to reduce the risk before placing the software product within the system or enclave. The ISSM must update the applicable system or enclave assessment and authorization documentation and hardware/software lists to reflect any solutions implemented. This update will be considered a "no security impact" modification to the system authorization.

2. Reciprocity. For products not already assessed via the RMF or the AF SACA process, the Enterprise AO allows ISSMs to use software products that are certified by another DoD AO or SCA. A list of recognized sources can be found at <u>http://go.usa.gov/3vPDS</u>. These software products are considered assessed and require no additional formal test or evaluation, so long as the actual environment, use, and configuration aligns with the intended environment, use, and configuration documented in the assessment package. Compliance with this decision is contingent upon the following conditions:

2.1. The software product and major version is verified on one of the recognized sources.

2.2.   Prior to implementation, the system/enclave ISSM must implement any required mitigations to reduce the security risk.

2.3. The system/enclave ISSM must update their applicable RMF documentation and hardware/software lists to reflect any solutions implemented. This update will be considered a no security impact modification to the system authorization.

3. Software Products Excluded from AF SACA. The following software products must be submitted through the AF Enterprise AO processes:

3.1. Products whose main function is encryption, but does not have Federal Information Processing Standard 140-2 certification.

3.2. Software that does not have a vendor or sponsor responsible for developing security patches.

3.3. Software with immitigable Moderate (CAT II) or higher vulnerabilities.

3.4. Software that uses ports, protocols, or services not listed in the DoD Category Assurance List (CAL).

3.5. Unsupported freeware and shareware.

3.6. Open Source Software (OSS) with no configuration/software support plan.

3.7. IA or IA-enabled products/software (IAW CNSSP No. 11, *National Policy Governing the Acquisition of Information Assurance* (IA) *and IA-Enabled Information Technology Products*).

Attachment 3

FINANCIAL IMPROVEMENT AND AUDIT READINESS (FIAR) IT CONTROLS GUIDANCE (OPR: AF/FM)

1. PURPOSE.
The purpose of this publication is to articulate mandatory guidance necessary to help ensure AF FIAR systems (described below) are authorized in a manner that promotes AF audit readiness under the terms of DoD Comptroller [OUSD(C)] *Financial Improvement and Audit Readiness (FIAR) Guidance*.

2. SCOPE.
2.1. The scope of this attachment encompasses AF system authorization processes relating to all AF systems designated by SAF/FM as AF FIAR systems.
2.2. FIAR systems are defined as core financial systems, mixed-systems, non-financial systems, and micro-applications that support key financial processes (i.e., general ledger management, funds management, payment management, receivable management, and cost management). They include systems that are relevant to financial statement disclosures, and that must operate reliably to protect the integrity of financial statement assertions. The list below describes characteristics that place a system in-scope for FIAR:
• Controls within the system are identified as key controls in the internal controls assessment;
• Systems are used to generate or store original key supporting documentation;
• Reports generated by the system are utilized in the execution of key controls; or
• Systems are relied upon to perform material calculations (i.e., to compute payroll).
2.3. This attachment's scope does not encompass system authorization processes relating to non-FIAR systems, nor does it include the full range of cybersecurity controls required to protect the confidentiality, integrity and availability of AF systems and applications.

3. APPLICABILITY.
This publication applies to:
3.1. All AF FIAR systems. AF FIAR systems may include but are not limited to: information systems (enclaves, major applications), IT services (internal & external), and IT products (software, hardware, applications).
3.2. All financial or financially-related information that is processed, stored, displayed, and/or transmitted by AF FIAR systems.
3.3. All service level agreements that manage service provider audit readiness requirements.

4. RESPONSIBILITIES.
The following assignment of responsibility and delegation of authority are to be understood as *additions* to the Responsibilities outlined in Chapter 2, rather than *substitutions*.
4.1. SAF/FM CIO. The SAF/FM CIO will oversee:
4.1.1. Adherence of Internal Control over Financial System (ICOFS) risk assessments and continuous monitoring of all AF FIAR systems;
4.1.2. The design of FIAR-related key controls over all AF FIAR systems, as well as tests to ensure their continuous effectiveness.
4.1.3. Development of standard contract language for use in contracts to develop, modify, or support AF FIAR systems to ensure that financial reporting and financial information integrity requirements are properly reflected to meet statutory and regulatory requirements.

4.2. Program Manager (PM). PMs of AF FIAR systems will:

4.2.1. Ensure AF system development lifecycle (SDLC) requirements, relevant FIAR requirements, and required FIAR IT controls are explicitly addressed in contracts with vendors for developing, modifying, or supporting AF FIAR systems.

4.2.3.Manage the design, test, and effective implementation of FIAR-related controls over their respective AF systems.

4.2.4.Oversee the documentation of all controls that are relevant to their system or application in a form suitable for presentation to IT auditors.

4.2.5.Manage the continuous monitoring regimen of AF FIAR systems for which they have program management responsibility.

4.2.6.Manage the process through which the design and tests of effectiveness for programs they manage are properly executed and memorialized in eMASS, to include the collection and storage of evidentiary documents.

4.5.3.Coordinate their activities as required with financial and IT auditors.

4.3. Information Owner (IO). Owners of AF financial and financially-related information pertinent to the AF's consolidated financial audit will:

4.3.1. Establish standards, policies, and procedures for proper handling of their financial information consistent with FIAR guidance.

4.3.2. Coordinate with AF FIAR system owners; identify confidentiality, integrity and availability requirements to help ensure AF FIAR systems are properly categorized.

4.3.3. Coordinate on controls selection and implementation with FIAR system PMs, ISOs, and ISSMs.

4.3.4. Coordinate with AO, SCAs, ISSMs, and ISSOs in the authorization and continuous monitoring processes related to financial information.

4.4. Information System Owner (ISO). Owners of AF FIAR systems will:

4.4.1. Ensure AF FIAR systems under their purview are appropriately categorized.

4.4.2. Coordinate with owners of financial and financially-related information to ensure all financial information handling requirements are appropriately addressed.

4.4.3. Coordinate with all RMF representatives for the AF FIAR system to ensure finance and financially-related controls are properly designed and effectively implemented.

4.4.4. Coordinate with SAF/FM CIO or designee to ensure AF FIAR systems and controls are properly configured to support relevant financial processes.

4.5. Information Systems Security Engineer (ISSE). ISSEs associated with AF FIAR systems will:

4.5.1. Capture and refine FIAR IT control and financial business process requirements, and ensure such requirements are effectively integrated into IT through purposeful architecting, design, development, configuration, and test.

4.5.2.Employ generally accepted best practices when implementing financial and finance-related controls and processes within AF FIAR systems, including software engineering methodologies, system/security engineering principles, secure design, secure architecture, and secure coding techniques.

4.6. AO. AOs assigned to AF FIAR systems will:

4.6.1. Assess and accept the risk of any FIAR-related controls not properly designed and not operating effectively before authorizing such systems to process, store, display, or transmit financial or financially-related information.

4.6.2. Ensure the design and tests of effectiveness are properly executed and documented in eMASS, to include the collection and storage of evidentiary documents in support of audit/ FIAR requirements.

4.6.3. Coordinate with the SAF/FM CIO on authorization decisions that have POA&Ms associated with key FIAR controls as referenced in Appendix 1.

4.7. SCA/ SCAR/ ASCA. SCAs/SCARs/ASCAs of FIAR systems will:

4.7.1. Develop a plan to assess key FIAR controls to ensure controls are properly implemented.

4.7.2. Assess FIAR-related controls to determine if they are properly designed and operating effectively before recommending the AO authorize such systems to process, store, display, or transmit financial or financially-related information.

4.7.3. Advise PMs and system owners on measures that could improve the design and/or effectiveness of FIAR-related controls.

4.8. Information System Security Manager (ISSM). ISSMs for AF FIAR systems will:

4.8.1. Maintain the audit readiness of the system throughout its lifecycle.

4.8.2. Support the ISO and/or PM in implementing the RMF in a manner that satisfies IT audit requirements reflected in GAO-09-232G, *Federal Information System Controls Audit Manual (FISCAM)*.

4.8.3. Ensure all audit evidence and related documentation is current and accessible to financial and IT auditors.

4.8.4. Manage the identification and implementation of controls that are relevant to financial audits performed under the terms of DoD Comptroller [OUSD(C)]; leverage the results of prior inspections and audits, including risk assessments performed under OMB Circular A-123 (as revised), *Management's Responsibility for Internal Control*, to develop an understanding the financial controls applicable to their respective system/application environments.

4.8.5. Support the ISO/PM in implementing corrective actions identified in audit Notice of Finding and Recommendations (NFRs)/Notice of Findings (NOFs) and associated plan of action and milestones (POA&M).

4.8.6. Report and present any additions and/or modifications that significantly impact the audit readiness posture of AF FIAR systems. As necessary, conduct additional risk assessments and/or security testing in coordination with assigned SCAs/SCARs/ASCAs. Notify the ISO, PM, and AO if any significant changes occur that may affect the authorization for the system.

4.8.7. In support of annual reporting requirements associated with Internal Controls Over Financial Systems (ICOFS), develop a strategy for continuously monitoring the AF FIAR system and information environment for events and configuration changes impacting the audit readiness posture, and assess the quality of FIAR controls implementation against performance indicators such as security incidents, feedback from external audit agencies, and financial evaluations.

4.8.8. Document all controls relevant to the system or application in a form suitable for presentation to IT auditors.

4.9. Information System Security Officer (ISSO). ISSOs for AF FIAR systems will:

4.9.1. Implement and enforce all AF FIAR policies, procedures, and countermeasures using the guidance within this instruction and applicable financial controls publications (i.e., Reference DoD Comptroller [OUSD(C)]).

4.9.2. In coordination with the ISSM, implement controls relevant to financial audits performed under the terms of DoD Comptroller [OUSD(C)].

4.9.3. Ensure authorized users are not assigned incompatible duties when granted access to AF FIAR systems.

4.9.4. In coordination with the ISSM, maintain all IS authorized user access control documentation; ensure this documentation is kept current, maintained as audit evidence, and made readily accessible to financial and IT auditors.

4.9.5. In coordination with the ISO, PM, and IO ensure software, hardware, and firmware complies with appropriate financial and business process configuration guidelines.

4.9.6. In coordination with the ISSM, initiate protective or corrective measures when a financial incident or vulnerability is discovered; cooperate with the implementation of the POA&M.

5. PROCESS.

The following process descriptions are intended to augment the systems authorization process described in Chapter 3; this supplemental guidance is applicable as described above.

5.1. FIAR Considerations in RMF Step One, *Categorize System.*

5.1.1. IAW categorization guidance contained in CNSSI No. 1253 (Reference (e)) and NIST Special Publication 800-60, Volume 2 (Reference (f)), the baseline security categorization for AF FIAR systems, exclusive of special factors affecting confidentiality, integrity and availability, is, at a minimum, as follows:

Security Category = {(confidentiality, Low), (integrity, Moderate), (availability, Low)}

5.1.2. Special factors affecting confidentiality. Confidentiality impacts are generally associated with the sensitivity of specific AF projects' existence, programs, and/or technologies that might be revealed by unauthorized disclosure of financial information. If an AF FIAR system contains financial information pertaining to sensitive programmatic or technical information, the baseline confidentiality value may be raised to Moderate. If the existence of programs or technologies is classified, the baseline confidentiality value may be raised to High.

5.1.3. Special factors affecting integrity. Fraud and errors can affect the AF's image, and corrective actions are often disruptive to operations. Errors represent the greatest threat; if an AF FIAR system contains financial information, the integrity of which supports or is considered crucial to a key decision-making process, the baseline integrity value may be raised to High.

5.1.4. Special factors affecting availability. Permanent loss/unavailability of financial management information can temporarily cripple AF financial operations. If an AF FIAR system contains financial information, the temporary or permanent loss of which would result in a *serious* adverse effect on AF financial operations or assets, or other DoD or federal financial operations or assets, the baseline availability value may be raised to Moderate; e.g., the unavailability of a given application and/or it's information output could directly or indirectly trigger a potentially material erroneous financial event. If an AF FIAR system contains financial information, the temporary or permanent loss of which would result in *severe or catastrophic* adverse effect on AF financial operations or assets, or other DoD or federal government financial operations or assets, the baseline availability value may be raised to High, e.g., the unavailability of a given application and/or it's information output could directly or indirectly triggers erroneous financial events across multiple systems, and/or in a manner that is like to result in a material impact on financial reporting.

5.2 FIAR Considerations in RMF Step Two, *Select Security Controls.*

5.2.1. Many RMF controls and enhancements are identical, or very similar, to analogous FISCAM controls, but require supplementation. DoD's instantiation of RMF allows for supplementary overlays to be issued addressing such specific needs; these overlays levy requirements that modify the standard RMF control baselines. OSD developed one such overlay, *Supplemental Implementation Instruction for Systems Impacting Financial Statement Audit Readiness,* that is intended to be implemented by all DoD components and financial and financially-relevant systems. However, OSD's guidance allows for flexibility of implementation, stating:

"If during the audit readiness process it is determined that a FISCAM control technique is not key to addressing the control objectives, then the associated RMF/NIST security control would no longer be required for financial statement audit readiness purposes."

5.2.2. AF FIAR systems must apply the control baseline appropriate to each system's overall security categorization, and tailor the resulting controls as appropriate on a system-by-system basis. Controls may be added to address non-financial concerns (i.e., cybersecurity, operational), or intentionally not implemented to contain costs and allow functionality consistent with risk. Such decisions should be the result of a consultative process between IOs, ISOs, PMs, ISSMs, AOs, with a full appreciation for AF financial control objectives. Appendix 1 to this publication contains a list of controls that must be considered. ISSMs and ISSOs should take into consideration and leverage the results of prior inspections and audits, including risk assessments performed in support of OMB Circular A-123.

5.2.3. AF FIAR system PMs, ISOs, ISSMs, and ISSOs must additionally determine which FIAR controls are common to, and/or inherited by, their respective systems/applications. As noted in NIST SP 800-53 r4, the determination as to whether a security control is common or inherited is context-based, and cannot be characterized as common or inherited simply based on reviewing the language of the control.

Many FIAR systems will benefit from inheriting some of the controls from a common service provider; that is, their system or application receives protection from security controls (or portions of security controls) that are developed, implemented, assessed, authorized, and monitored by entities internal or external to the system/application's responsible organization.

5.2.4. AF FIAR system PMs and ISSM must document all controls relevant to the system or application in a form suitable for presentation to IT auditors. ISSMs should be able to describe in detail which controls are the responsibility of the program, which are shared between the program and an external service provider, and which are inherited from an external service provider.

5.3. FIAR Considerations in RMF Step Three, *Implement Security Controls.* Effective AF FIAR control implementation requires the controls be properly designed, implemented, and operated.

5.3.1. Security Control Design: Proper control design is demonstrated by an architecture of guidance and documentation that includes:

A specific description of the control as it is applies to the system/application environment, including identification of the responsible person(s)/organization(s);

Identification of governing local, AF, and/or DoD plans and policies;

Identification of relevant technical, operational, or behavioral standards; and

Documented procedures addressing the steps for implementing and monitoring the control.

All design documentation must be in final form; documents in draft form will not be considered authoritative for audit purposes.

5.3.2. Security Control Implementation: Proper control implementation is demonstrated by provision of evidentiary materials that prove the control is in place and operating effectively. Evidentiary matter can include but is not limited to:

Meeting minutes

Organizations emails

Populated decision matrices

Formal (i.e., signed and dated) forms, reports, and decision papers

Configuration management records

System logs

Recent operational system records/dumps

Reconciliation records

5.4. FIAR Considerations in RMF Step Four, *Assess Security Controls.* Generally accepted financial audit methodology provides standard procedures for testing both control design and control effectiveness.

5.4.1. Tests of Design (TOD). TOD procedures are performed first; if TOD tests are not passed, the control may be failed in its entirety at the auditor's discretion.

5.4.2. Tests of Effectiveness (TOE). If TOD tests are passed, auditors will execute TOE procedures to assess whether the control is operating as designed and effective in its operation. Should a control not pass TOE, the control will be failed; auditor discretion will be applied to determine the severity of the failure.

5.4.3. Creating, Maintaining, and Presenting Evidence.

5.4.3.1. Evidentiary matter need only supply sufficient evidence of a given control's effectiveness and management's due diligence in continuous monitoring. It is neither required nor desired that evidence be created for no other purpose, or embellished past the point of management's legitimate needs.

5.4.3.2. Evidence will be maintained in the eMASS system of record. eMASS provides a venue for organizing and storing digital information; however, some evidence does not lend itself to digital storage and may be best preserved in hard copy.

5.4.3.3. Some evidentiary records must be created on an ad hoc basis at the auditor's request. PMs, ISOs, and ISSM's should coordinate with the audit team as early as possible to gain an understanding of such possible requests.

5.4.4. Minimizing the impact of audit investigations on mission operations requires pre-audit and pre-interview coordination between the PM, ISSM, and audit team.

5.4.4.1. PMs should expect to receive a request from the audit team for evidentiary documents in the form of a Document Request List (DRL) or Provided By Client (PBC) request, and be prepared to respond in a timely manner. (*Average allotted time to provide evidence is 2 weeks from date PBC is received by the AF team*).

5.4.4.2. PMs should coordinate with the audit team to help ensure interview objectives are clearly articulated by the auditor in order to limit the need for multiple interviews on the same subject and ensure all relevant/knowledgeable system/application personnel are available during the interview.

5.4.4.3. PMs should coordinate with the audit team to help ensure all DRL/PBC requests are satisfied at least 1 day prior to interviews.

5.5. FIAR Considerations in RMF Step Five, *Authorize the System.*

5.5.1. AF FIAR system AOs must obtain the advice and consent of a designated SAF/FM CIO or designated representative before issuing an authorization decision for an AF FIAR system.

5.5.2 FM ISO's coordination on authorization decisions must be formally signed and retained.

5.6. FIAR Considerations in RMF Step Six, *Monitor Security Controls*. AF FIAR system control monitoring will take place both in-process and periodically through internal reviews and external inspections.

5.6.1. AF FIAR systems will be configured to preserve AF financial information's integrity to the greatest extent practical. AF FIAR system ISSOs must configure their respective systems/applications to automatically identify and handle error conditions in an expeditious manner without providing information that could be exploited by adversaries. Examples of automated integrity functions include, but are not limited to:

Batch totals

Sequence checking

Reconciliations

Control totals

5.6.2 AF FIAR PMs must develop and implement management procedures to identify and correct errors that occur during data entry and processing. Error handling procedures must provide reasonable assurance that errors and irregularities are detected, reported, and corrected. This audit and monitoring capability should include:

User error logs to provide timely follow-up and correction of unresolved data errors and irregularities,

An established monitoring process to assure the effectiveness of error handling procedures, and

Procedures to periodically review user error logs to determine the extent to which data errors are being made, and the status of uncorrected data errors.

5.6.3.AF FIAR system PMs must initiate prompt action to correct deficiencies identified through internal monitoring or external inspection. This includes maintenance of a formal POA&M, as well as procedures to:

Ensure the accuracy of POA&M information.

Prioritize POA&M items based on cost, level of complexity, risk, and impact on the financial statement.

Determine whether control weaknesses identified through IT audits are included in the POA&Ms, and, if not, determining the cause.

Ensure the timely resolution of identified deficiencies. OMB Circular A-123 recommends audit remediation items be addressed within 6 months.

6. FM Control Implementation Guidance.

The RMF process is similar to the DoD C&A process it replaced, but the scope of 'risk management' is substantially greater. While the former process was sharply focused on IT risk, the RMF encompasses both IT risk and business risk, and tends DoD program managers (PMs) to a more varied view of risk that can be continuously monitored at both program and enterprise levels.

This is a favorable development for DoD's financial managers, as the RMF controls baseline aligns more closely with the controls precepts and baselines that are intended to protect the integrity of financial information and processes as expressed in the Government Accountability Office (GAO) Federal Information System Controls Audit Manual (FISCAM). Viewed broadly, RMF controls accord with financial substantially, although not completely; in other words, successfully executing the RMF process is tantamount to satisfying most, but not all of the IT general controls in the FISCAM control baseline.

As the AF transitions to the new system authorization process, the AF decided to leverage the RMF to achieve AF financial audit readiness as directed by DoD Comptroller guidance, Financial Improvement and Audit Readiness (FIAR). To this end, Secretary of the Air Force/ Financial Management (SAF/FM) developed financial management (FM) supplemental guidance to augment and extend the RMF controls baseline to fully address all financial and financially relevant controls. This control guidance is intended to be used in conjunction with the RMF process as it is applied to AF financial and financially-related IT, the goal being to use the RMF process to satisfy cybersecurity and FISCAM controls guidance simultaneously.

The Appendix below presents a list of controls that SAF/FM determined to be mandatory for all AF FIAR systems, as well as a list of controls that SAF/FM determined as candidates for tailoring-out on a system-by-system basis.

As noted above in section 2, the controls presented in the appendix relate to securing financial information, and do not encompass the full range of cybersecurity controls that may be required to attain an unqualified ATO.

Appendix 1 to Attachment 3
AF FIAR SYSTEM MANDATORY AND TAILORABLE AF FINANCIAL CONTROLS
This Appendix presents all controls that are or may be applicable to AF FIAR systems. These include both controls presented in NIST SP 800-60 volume 2, as well as additional controls that SAF/FM determined to be mandatory for implementation in AF FIAR systems. Controls that SAF/FM determined to be of insufficient relevance to the AF Financial statement, or which are likely to prove uneconomic or operationally infeasible, are so indicated as 'Tailorable' in the Appendix column titled "Control Ranking", so long as those controls are not specified as mandatory for connection to the AFIN. At the discretion of the pertinent AO, controls so indicated can be tailored out of AF FIAR systems' control baselines for the purposes of financial reporting. However, nothing presented in this Appendix is intended to preclude control implementations that are required for cybersecurity or operational purposes.

The complete list of financial management overlay controls can be found here.

BY ORDER OF THE SECRETARY
OF THE AIR FORCE

AIR FORCE POLICY DIRECTIVE 17-1

12 APRIL 2016

Cyberspace

INFORMATION DOMINANCE
GOVERNANCE AND MANAGEMENT

COMPLIANCE WITH THIS PUBLICATION IS MANDATORY

ACCESSIBILITY: Publications and forms are available on the e-Publishing website at
www.e-Publishing.af.mil for downloading or ordering

RELEASABILITY: There are no releasability restrictions on this publication

---

OPR: SAF/CIO A6SS

Supersedes: AFPD 33-2, 3 August 2011;
AFPD 33-4, 17 January 2013;
AFPD 33-5, 11 January 2013

Certified by: SAF/CIO A6
(Lt Gen William J. Bender)
Pages: 15

This Air Force (AF) Policy Directive (PD) establishes AF policy for the governance and management of activities to achieve Information Dominance under the direction of the Chief of Information Dominance and Chief Information Officer (SAF/CIO A6). Information Dominance is defined as the operational advantage gained from the ability to collect, control, exploit, and defend information to optimize decision making and maximize warfighting effects. This directive implements: Office of Management and Budget (OMB) Circular A-11, *Preparation, Submission, and Execution of the Budget*; OMB Circular A-130, *Management of Federal Information Resources*; OMB Memorandum M-11-29, *Chief Information Officer Authorities*; Department of Defense (DoD) Directive (DoDD) 3700.01, *DoD Command and Control (C2) Enabling Capabilities*; DoDD 7045.20, *Capability Portfolio Management*; DoDD 8000.01, *Management of the Department of Defense Information Enterprise.* DoDD 8115.01 *Information Technology Portfolio Management*; DoDD 8220.1, *Single Agency Manager (SAM) for Pentagon Information Technology Services (ITS)*; DoDD 8521.01, *Department of Defense Biometrics*; 8140.01, *Cyberspace Workforce Management*; DoD Instruction (DoDI) O-3780.01, *Senior Leader Secure Communications Modernization (SLSCM)*; DoDI S-4660.04, *Encryption of Imagery Transmitted by Airborne Systems and Unmanned Aircraft Control Communications*; DoDI S-5100.92, *Defense and National Leadership Command Capability (DNLCC) Governance*; DoDI 5205.8, *Access to Classified Cryptographic Information*; DoDI 5205.13, *Defense Industrial Base (DIB) Cyber Security/ Information Assurance (CS/IA) Activities*; DoDI 8115.02 *Information Technology Portfolio Management Implementation*; DoDI 8310.01, *Information Technology Standards in the DoD*; DoDI 8320.05, *Electromagnetic Spectrum Data*

Sharing; DoDI 8330.01, *Interoperability of Information Technology (IT) and National Security Systems (NSS)*; DoDI 8510.01, *Risk Management Framework (RMF) for DoD Information Technology (IT)*.

This directive is consistent with: Subtitle III of Title 40 of the Clinger-Cohen Act (CCA) of 1996, National Defense Authorization Act (NDAA) 2005 § 2222, NDAA 2009 (PL110-417) § 908, NDAA 2010 § 1072, NDAA 2010 § 804, NDAA 2012 § 901 and NDAA 2015; Federal Information Security Management Act (FISMA), 44 USC Chap 35, Subchap II; Title 10, USC, Section 2223(b) Information Technology: *Additional Responsibilities of Chief Information Officers of Military Department, 2007;* DoDD 5000.01, *The Defense Acquisition System*; DoDD 5144.02, *DoD Chief Information Officer (DoD CIO)*; DoDI 5000.02, *Operation of the Defense Acquisition System*; DoDI 5200.44, *Protection of Mission Critical Functions to Achieve Trusted Systems and Networks;* CJCSI 5116.05, *Military Command, Control, Communications, and Computers Executive Board*; and CJCSI 5123.01G, *Charter of the Joint Requirements Oversight Council*.

This directive applies to all military and civilian AF personnel, members of the AF Reserve, Air National Guard, and individuals or organizations authorized by an appropriate government official to manage any portion of the AF Information Network (AFIN). It applies to all information, information systems (IS), and cyberspace and information technology (IT) infrastructure within AF purview. Comments and recommended changes regarding this publication should be sent through appropriate channels using AF Form 847, Recommendation for Change of Publication, to the office of primary responsibility (OPR), SAF/A6SS, **usaf.pentagon.saf-cio-a6.mbx.a6ss-workflow@mail.mil.** Ensure that all records created as a result of processes prescribed in this publication are maintained in accordance with AF Manual (AFMAN) 33-363, Management of Records, and disposed of in accordance with AF Records Disposition Schedule (RDS) located in the AF Records Information Management System (AFRIMS).

SUMMARY OF CHANGES

This AFPD, published along with AFPD 17-2, supersedes AFPD 33-4, AFPD 33-5, and those portions of AFPD 33-2 not superseded by AFPD 17-2. This directive aligns and consolidates policies on cyberspace and IT management with current AF doctrine, statutory, and regulatory guidelines.

1. Overview. This directive establishes the AF policy for information dominance governance and management to provide a process for the SAF/CIO A6 to fulfill the duties of the AF CIO established in federal laws and DoD issuances. This directive provides a means by which the AF will cross-functionally align cyberspace programs and capabilities to effectively and efficiently deliver capabilities to users. Cyberspace is defined as a global domain within the information environment consisting of the interdependent network of IT infrastructures and resident data, including the Internet, telecommunications networks, computer systems, and embedded processors and controllers.

2. Policy. The AF will:

2.1. Develop cyberspace capabilities to execute, enhance and support Joint, Coalition, and AF core missions, by rapidly developing and implementing innovative solutions, and when appropriate, leveraging commercial products/services to deliver AF capabilities in a Disconnected, Intermittent, Low-Bandwidth environment.

2.2. Deliver cyberspace capabilities to support the four defined DoD mission areas: Warfighting (WMA), Business (BMA), Information Environment (IEMA), and Defense Intelligence (DIMA).

2.3. Optimize the planning, programming, budgeting, and execution of cyberspace investments consistent with national, DoD, Joint and AF policy.

2.4. Establish and track performance measures for cyberspace investments, programs, and acquisitions to ensure compliance with validated requirements.

2.5. Design, develop, incorporate, test, and evaluate all AF IT, to include Platform IT (PIT), and NSS for interoperability and supportability, and as necessary, determine tradeoffs among mission effectiveness, cybersecurity, efficiency, survivability, resiliency, and IT interoperability.

2.6. Ensure cyberspace capabilities are designed to enhance information sharing, collaboration, and situational awareness, consistent with cybersecurity standards and best practices.

3. Responsibilities. The responsibilities for cyberspace and IT are overseen by SAF/CIO A6 and shared among numerous key stakeholders. CIO responsibilities are codified in Title 10, USC § 2223a and 8014; Title 40, USC, Subtitle III; and, Title 44, USC § 3506. Acquisition authority is codified in Title 10, USC § 1704 and 8014. Chief Financial Officer authority is codified in Title 10, USC § 8022. Chief Management Officer and Deputy Chief Management Officer authorities are in Title 10, USC § 2222, and Public Law 110-417, § 908 (NDAA 2009).

3.1. **Under Secretary of the Air Force.** As Chief Management Officer, provide any determinations required for defense business systems under Title 10, USC § 2222.

3.2. **Chief of Information Dominance and Chief Information Officer (SAF/CIO A6).** SAF/CIO A6 has a wide range of responsibilities which are listed in detail in the SAF/CIO A6 Mission Directive (AFMD 1-26). These responsibilities may be summarized as follows::

3.2.1. Set the strategic direction for fully exploiting cyberspace by leading Air Staff-level executive groups and boards in the development of policies, strategies, roadmaps, and technical baselines.

3.2.1.1. Charter AF cyberspace governance and Warfighting Integration forums and, in coordination with the Core Function Leads (CFLs), appoint representatives to cyberspace governance forums external to the AF.

3.2.2. Execute all responsibilities and functions outlined in statutes, directives, and regulations pertaining to an Agency Chief Information Officer or military department CIO.

3.2.3. Develop and implement a deliberate budget and investment review and approval process, within existing corporate processes, to integrate cyberspace requirements and investments across all mission areas.

3.2.4. Ensure an operationally resilient, reliable, interoperable, and secure AF Information Network to meet the needs of AF core missions and AF responsibilities for Joint and Coalition Operations.

3.2.5. Serve as the Functional Authority for military and civilian IT, cyberspace, and information management career fields for the life cycle program management of IT and cyberspace capabilities.

3.2.6. For all acquisitions subject to DoDI 5000.02, review and approve the Cybersecurity Strategy for acquisitions of systems containing IT prior to milestone decisions or contract award. For ACAT ID, IAM, and IAC programs, forward the Cybersecurity Strategy to the DoD CIO for review and approval. For SAP systems, conduct the review in coordination with SAF/AA. For nuclear systems, conduct the review in coordination with AF/A10.

3.2.7. Oversee, establish, integrate and maintain the target baseline (TB) and implementation baseline (IB) in coordination with appropriate governance forums.

3.3. Deputy Chief of Staff for Intelligence, Surveillance, and Reconnaissance (AF/A2) will:

3.3.1. Advocate for a prioritized integration of battlespace awareness warfighting systems and intelligence, surveillance, and reconnaissance (ISR) enterprise interoperability under the Warfighting Integration governance forums and with other appropriate forums as needed.

3.3.2. Participate in cyberspace governance forums.

3.3.3. Coordinate and facilitate the review of DIMA cyberspace capabilities and investment.

3.3.4. Identify opportunities to share capabilities and investment between DIMA and the other mission areas.

3.3.5. Coordinate intelligence activities required to fully characterize the cyber threat.

3.3.5.1. Facilitate the provision of cyber intelligence data for acquisition development programs.

3.3.5.2. Facilitate the provision of cyber intelligence data to support modeling and simulation (M&S) and test and evaluation (T&E) activities.

3.4. Deputy Chief of Staff for Operations (AF/A3) will:

3.4.1. Advocate for the integration of cyberspace capabilities into AF operational capabilities-based planning and development processes in coordination with the Cyberspace Superiority Core Function Lead (CFL).

3.4.2. Participate in cyberspace governance forums and identify mission assurance requirements and priorities for all phases of operations.

3.4.3. Coordinate and facilitate the review of cyberspace capabilities through the Warfighting Integration governance forums.

3.5. **The Deputy Chief of Staff for Strategic Plans and Requirements (A5/8)** will:

3.5.1. Be responsible for AF Joint Capabilities Integration and Development System planning and requirements development processes and procedures for cyberspace capabilities.

3.5.2. Collaborate with Cyberspace Superiority CFL, MAJCOMs, other Services, and the defense S&T community to support future AF cyberspace capabilities development through concept development and experimentation.

3.5.3. Ensure program funding is aligned with the validated requirement for each acquisition phase.

3.5.4. Participate in cyberspace governance forums.

3.6. **Air Force, Director of Test and Evaluation (AF/TE)** will:

3.6.1. Participate in cyberspace governance forums and identify T&E requirements.

3.6.2. Develop and implement a comprehensive test strategy that includes cyber testing, and institute T&E policy consistent with AF and DoD policies.

3.6.3. Provide guidance, direction, and oversight of all AF T&E activities, including integration of cyber test, throughout program lifecycle.

3.6.4. Ensure AF T&E infrastructure utilizes latest cyber intelligence data to provide an operationally representative cyber environment for T&E.

3.7. **The Administrative Assistant to the Secretary of the Air Force (SAF/AA)** will:

3.7.1. IAW AFPD 16-14, *Security Enterprise Governance*, provide assistance to SAF/CIO A6 in the presentation and vetting of cyberspace issues and agenda items to the Air Force Security Enterprise Executive Board when appropriate.

3.7.2. On behalf of the security enterprise and special access program (SAP) community, participate in cyberspace governance forums.

3.7.3. As the Senior Security Official and Security Program Executive, ensure Personnel, Information, Industrial, and Insider Threat security programs are aligned with and support cyberspace policy and execution.

3.7.4. Support the SAF/CIO A6 in execution of CIO responsibilities for Special Access Program networks.

3.8. **Assistant Secretary of the Air Force for Acquisition (SAF/AQ)** will:

3.8.1. Participate in cyberspace governance forums.

3.8.2. Work with SAF/CIO A6 to ensure AF cyber acquisition programs are consistent with the Information Dominance Flight Plan and the AF Enterprise Architecture developed by SAF/CIO A6.

3.8.3. Ensure the execution of AF acquisition and sustainment programs appropriately implement cyberspace and warfighting integration requirements, including;

interoperability, reusability of application designs; and promoting the adoption of IT as common services and the AF common computing environment. These requirements will be implemented IAW AFPD 63-1/20-1, *Integrated Life Cycle Management*.

3.8.4. Ensure compliance with Electromagnetic Environmental Effects control and anti-tamper requirements during the acquisition of AF cyber systems.

3.8.5. Ensure the acquisition program office Program Manager is responsible for cybersecurity of the weapon system, to include IT interfaces and embedded computer hardware and software, and has allocated sufficient resources to cybersecurity.

3.8.6. Ensure all acquisition programs plan and conduct robust developmental and operational cyber testing prior to system deployment.

3.8.7. Designate DoD/AF information systems that the AF Service Acquisition Executive has determined are critical to the direct fulfillment of military or intelligence missions as "applicable systems" in accordance with DoDI 5200.44, *Protection of Mission Critical Functions to Achieve Trusted Systems and Networks*.

3.9. **Assistant Secretary of the Air Force, Financial Management and Comptroller (SAF/FM)** will:

3.9.1. Coordinate, as required, on business case analysis and economic analysis supporting cyberspace requirements.

3.9.2. In accordance with 10 USC § 8022, approve and supervise all financial cyberspace programs to ensure compliance with finance and accounting standards.

3.9.3. Participate in cyberspace governance forums.

3.10. **Director of Business Transformation and Deputy Chief Management Officer (SAF/MG)** will:

3.10.1. Coordinate and facilitate the cross-functional review of AF Defense Business Systems (DBS) and support the USecAF as the business systems Pre-Certification Authority through the Enterprise Senior Working Group.

3.10.2. Coordinate the development of business enterprise architecture, including the capture of business processes and supporting AF DBS.

3.10.3. Participate in cyberspace governance forums.

3.10.4. Be responsible for the Service Development and Delivery Process for development of Defense Business System requirements and capabilities.

3.11. **Air Force Space Command (AFSPC)** will:

3.11.1. Serve as lead command for AF cyberspace operations and Cyberspace Superiority CFL.

3.11.2. Develop the Cyberspace Superiority Core Function Support Plan aligned with the AF Information Dominance Flight Plan and IEMA roadmap developed by SAF/CIO A6.

3.11.3. Participate in cyberspace governance forums.

3.11.4. Establish capability needs and requirements for cyberspace infrastructure within the Cyberspace Superiority CFL portfolio.

3.11.5. Develop and maintain the AF Operational Baseline (OB) which is synchronized with the Target Baseline (TB) and Implementation Baseline (IB) developed by SAF/CIO A6.

3.11.6. Deploy AF approved cyber weapon systems.

3.11.7. In conjunction with the National Security Agency, provide oversight and guidance for AF COMSEC, AF Cryptologic Modernization and the development, fielding and sustainment of cryptologic solutions within the AF.

3.11.8. Develop a trained, educated, experienced force to conduct cyberspace operations.

3.12. Air Force Materiel Command will:

3.12.1. Serve as the core functional lead integrator for agile combat support.

3.12.2. Conduct technological research and materiel development activities to acquire, perform developmental testing of, field and sustain current and future cyberspace capabilities.

3.13. **CFLs** will:

3.13.1. Plan and program cyberspace investments for assigned service core functions based on the AF Strategic Master Plan and IDFP, the IEMA Roadmap, and other IDFP-aligned roadmaps.

3.13.2. Coordinate with cyberspace governance forums and to enhance collaborative efforts potentially reducing costs, complexity, and unnecessary duplication of effort.

3.13.3. Establish mission capability needs and requirements for cyberspace infrastructure within the respective CFL portfolio.

3.13.4. Provide investment performance information to SAF/CIO A6.

3.13.5. Serve as the Functional Sponsor for Defense Business System requirements within the Service Development and Delivery Process leading into the Defense Acquisition System.

3.14. **All HAF Functionals, MAJCOMs, DRUs, and FOAs** will:

3.14.1. Participate in the cyberspace governance forums, as required. Identify new cyberspace requirements to responsible CFL.

3.14.2. Ensure all cyberspace investments are identified and registered in the SAF/CIO A6-directed management control system.

3.14.3. Maintain enterprise architectures for their areas of responsibility, to include mission-unique IS solution architectures, and be able to integrate their architectural data using AF-directed repositories.

3.14.4. Develop and exercise contingency plans for mission assurance when operating under conditions of diminished or denied NSS, mission critical IT and data availability.

3.14.5. Identify and advocate for rapid innovation initiatives, both leveraging cyberspace capabilities and operating through cyberspace.

3.14.6. Ensure that subordinate organizations identify the Protection Level of their cyber and computer/communications assets and apply integrated defense measures IAW AFI 31-101, *Integrated Defense*.

3.15. The General Counsel (SAF/GC) and The Judge Advocate General (AF/JA) will advise the AF on legal matters related to information dominance governance and management.

4. Applicability to ISR and Counterintelligence Authorities and Policies. Nothing in this directive shall alter or supersede the existing authorities and policies of the Director of National Intelligence (DNI) regarding the protection of Sensitive Compartmented Information (SCI) or intelligence SAPs. The application of the provisions and procedures of this directive to SCI or other intelligence ISs is encouraged where they may complement or address areas not otherwise specifically addressed. AF ISR and counterintelligence governance, compliance, and reporting is governed by applicable Attorney General, DNI, Under Secretary of Defense (Intelligence), Director of Central Intelligence, and Director, National Security Agency directives and guidelines.

DEBORAH L. JAMES
Secretary of the Air Force

Attachment 1

GLOSSARY OF REFERENCES AND SUPPORTING INFORMATION

References

Title 10, USC, Section 2223(b), *"Information Technology: Additional Responsibilities of Chief Information Officers of Military Department,* 2007

Title 44, USC, Section 3541, *Federal Information Security Management Act (FISMA)*, 2002

National Defense Authorization Act (NDAA), Published Annually

Clinger-Cohen Act (CCA), 1996

OMB Circular A-11, *Preparation, Submission, and Execution of the Budget,* August 3, 2012

OMB Circular A-130, *Management of Federal Information Resources,* November 28, 2000

OMB Memorandum M-11-29, *Chief Information Officer Authorities,* August 8, 2011

NIST Special Publication 800-59, *Guideline for Identifying an Information System as a National Security System,* August 2003

DoDD 3700.01, *DoD Command and Control (C2) Enabling Capabilities*, October 22, 2014

DoDD 5000.01, *The Defense Acquisition System,* May 12, 2003

DoDD 5144.02, *DoD Chief Information Officer (DoD CIO)*, November 21, 2014

DoDD 7045.20, *Capability Portfolio Management*, September 25, 2008;

DoDD 8000.01, *Management of the Department of Defense Information Enterprise,* February 10, 2009

DoDD 8115.01, *Information Technology Portfolio Management,* October 10, 2005

DoDD 8140.01, Cyberspace Workforce Management, August 11, 2015

DoDD 8521.01E, *Department of Defense Biometrics*, February 21, 2008

DoDI O-3780.01, *Senior Leader Secure Communications Modernization (SLSCM)*, May 22, 2014

DoDI S-4460.01, *Encryption of Imagery Transmitted by Airborne Systems and Unmanned Aircraft Control Communications*, July 27, 2011

DoDI 5000.02, *Operation of the Defense Acquisition System*, January 7, 2015

DoDI S-5100.92, *Defense and National Leadership Command Capability (DNLCC) Governance*, May 11, 2009

DoDI S-5200.16, *Objectives and Minimum Standards for Communications Security (COMSEC) Measures Used in Nuclear Command and Control (NC2) Communications (U)*, November 14, 2007;

DoDI 5200.44, *Protection of Mission Critical Functions to Achieve Trusted Systems and Networks,* November 5, 2012;

DoDI 5205.8, *Access to Classified Cryptographic Information*, November 8, 2007;

DoDI 8115.02, *Information Technology Portfolio Management Implementation*, October 30, 2006

DoDD 8220.1, *Single Agency Manager (SAF) for Pentagon Information Technology Services (ITS)*, March 1, 1995;

DoDI 8310.01, *Information Technology Standards in the DoD*, February 2, 2015

DoDI 8320.05, *Electromagnetic Spectrum Data Sharing*, August 18, 2011

DoDI 8330.01, *Interoperability of Information Technology (IT), including National Security Systems (NSS)*, May 21, 2014

DoDI 8500.01, *Cybersecurity*, March 14, 2014

DoDI 8510.01, *Risk Management Framework (RMF) for DoD Information Technology (IT)*, March 12, 2014

CJCSI 5116.05, *Military Command, Control, Communications, and Computers Executive Board*, April 23, 2014

CJCSI 5123.01G Charter of the Joint Requirements Oversight Council, February 12, 2015

JP 3-12, *Cyberspace Operations*, February 5, 2013

AFPD 16-14, *Security Enterprise Governance*, July 24, 2014

AFI 31-101, *Integrated Defense*, October 8, 2009

AFI 38-101, *Air Force Organization*, March 16, 2011

AFMAN 33-363, *Management of Records,* March 1, 2008

AF Information Dominance Flight Plan (IDFP), v2.0, May 1, 2015

Prescribed Forms

None

Adopted Forms

AF Form 847, *Recommendation for Change of Publication*

Abbreviations and Acronyms

AF —Air Force

AFI—Air Force Instruction

AFIN—Air Force Information Network

AFMAN—Air Force Manual

AFPD—Air Force Policy Directive

AFRIMS—Air Force Records Information Management System

AFSPC—Air Force Space Command

BMA —Business Mission Area

C2—Command and Control

CCA—Clinger-Cohen Act

CFL—Core Function Lead

CIO—Chief Information Officer

DBS—Defense Business System

DCMO—Deputy Chief Management Officer

DoD—Department of Defense

DoDD—Department of Defense Directive

DoDI—Department of Defense Instruction

DIMA —Defense Intelligence Mission Area

DRU—Direct Report Units

EA—Enterprise Architecture

FISMA—Federal Information Security Management Act

FOA—Field Operating Agency

HAF—Headquarters Air Force

IB—Implementation Baseline

IDFP —Information Dominance Flight Plan

IEMA —Information Environment Mission Area

IS —Information System

ISR—Intelligence, Surveillance, and Reconnaissance

IT—Information Technology

ITIL—Information Technology Infrastructure Library

MAJCOM—Major Command

NDAA—National Defense Authorization Act

NSS—National Security System

OB—Operational Baseline

OMB—Office of Management and Budget

OPR—Office of Primary Responsibility

PEO—Program Executive Officer

PIT —Platform Information Technology

RDS—Records Disposition Schedule

SCF—Service Core Function

T&E —Test and Evaluation

TB—Target Baseline

USC —United States Code

USecAF —Undersecretary of the Air Force

Terms

AF Information Network (AFIN) — The globally interconnected, end-to-end set of AF information capabilities, and associated processes for collecting, processing, storing, disseminating, and managing information on-demand to AF warfighters, policy makers, and support personnel, including owned and leased communications and computing systems and services, software (including applications), data, security services, other associated services, and national security systems." (Derived from the JP 3-12 definition of DoDIN).

Business Mission Area (BMA)—The BMA ensures that the right capabilities, resources, and materiel are reliably delivered to our warfighters: what they need, where they need it, when they need it, anywhere in the world. In order to cost-effectively meet these requirements, the DoD current business and financial management infrastructure - processes, systems, and data standards - are being transformed to ensure better support to the warfighter and improve accountability to the taxpayer. Integration of business transformation for the DoD business enterprise is led by the Deputy Secretary of Defense in his role as the Chief Operating Officer of the Department. (DoDI 8115.02).

Core Function Lead—SecAF/CSAF-appointed senior leader responsible for specific Core Functions (CF) providing AF-level, long-term views. CFLs integrate Total Force concepts, capabilities, modernization, and resourcing to ensure future assigned core capabilities across the range of military operations as directed by AF Strategy and Strategic Planning Guidance. CFLs are responsible for the Core Function Support Plan and recommendations for the development of the POM for the assigned CF. CFLs have tasking authority regarding CF issues to identify enabling capabilities and integration requirements/opportunities. (AFPD 90-11).

Cybersecurity—Prevention of damage to, protection of, and restoration of computers, electronic communications systems, electronic communications services, wire communication, and electronic communication, including information contained therein, to ensure its availability, integrity, authentication, confidentiality, and nonrepudiation. (DoDI 8500.01).

Cyberspace—A global domain within the information environment consisting of the interdependent network of information technology infrastructures and resident data, including the Internet, telecommunications networks, computer systems, and embedded processors and controllers. (Joint Pub 3-12) NOTE: synonymous with cyber when used as an adjective.

Defense Intelligence Mission Area (DIMA)—The DIMA includes IT investments within the Military Intelligence Program and Defense component programs of the National Intelligence Program. The USD(I) has delegated responsibility for managing the DIMA portfolio to the Director, Defense Intelligence Agency, but USD(I) retains final signature authority. DIMA management will require coordination of issues among portfolios that extend beyond the Department of Defense to the overall Intelligence Community. (DoDI 8115.02).

Enterprise Architecture (EA)—The explicit description and documentation of the current and desired relationships among business and management processes and supporting resources (e.g., IT, personnel). It describes the "current architecture" and "target architecture," to include the rules, standards, and systems life cycle information to optimize and maintain the environment which the agency wishes to create and maintain by managing its IT portfolio. The EA must also provide a strategy that will enable the agency to support its current state and also act as the roadmap for transition to its target environment. These transition processes will include an agency's capital planning and investment control processes, agency EA planning processes, and agency systems life cycle methodologies. The EA will define principles and goals and set direction on such issues as the promotion of interoperability, open systems, public access, compliance with Government Paperwork Elimination Act, end user satisfaction, and IT security. The agency must support the EA with a complete inventory of agency information resources, including personnel, equipment, and funds devoted to information resources management and information technology, at an appropriate level of detail.

Governance—Governance is the framework of rules and practices that ensures continuity, collaboration, and de-confliction of interests across an organization to clearly define policies, processes, and investments. (IDFP V2.0).

Implementation Baseline (IB)—The Implementation Baseline is the baseline of acquisition selected products and their informed/allowed configurations that implement the architecture, standards and protocols, and guidelines specified in the Target Baseline. The Implementation Baseline informs the Operational Baseline of the acquisition selected products and how they are to be configured to support deployment of user applications across the infrastructure topology. The Implementation Baseline governs the implementation of the Development and Integration/Test environments.

Information Dominance —The operational advantage gained from the ability to collect, control, exploit, and defend information to optimize decision making and maximize warfighting effects. (AF Information Dominance Strategy).

Information Environment — The aggregate of individuals, organizations, and systems that collect, process, disseminate, or act on information. (JP 3-13).

Information Environment Mission Area (IEMA)—IEMA is the DoD information (IT) portfolio that manages investments in the current and future integrated information sharing, computing and communications environment of the Global Information Grid (GIG). The IE comprises GIG assets that operate as, provide information transport for, perform enterprise management of, and assure various levels and segments of the enterprise network, ranging from local area to wide area networks and from tactical to operational and strategic networks. The domains are Communications, Computing Infrastructure, Core Enterprise Services, and Information Assurance. (DoDI 8115.02).

Information System (IS)—A discrete set of information resources organized for the collection, processing, maintenance, use, sharing, dissemination, or disposition of information. (44 U.S.C. Sec 3502).

Information Technology (IT)—Any equipment, or interconnected system or subsystem of equipment, that is used in the automatic acquisition, storage, manipulation, management, movement, control, display, switching, interchange, transmission, or reception of data or information by the executive agency. This includes equipment used by a Component directly, or used by a contractor under a contract with the Component, which (i) requires the use of such equipment, or (ii) requires the use, to a significant extent, of such equipment in the performance of a service or the furnishing of a product. The term "IT" also includes computers, ancillary equipment, software, firmware and similar procedures, services (including support services), and related resources. Notwithstanding the above, the term "IT" does not include any equipment that is required by a Federal contractor incidental to a Federal contract. Note: The above term is considered synonymous with the term "information system" as defined and used in AF programs. The term "IT" does not include National Security Systems (NSS) according to 44 USC 3502.

IT Portfolio Management (Portfolio management)—The management of selected groupings of IT resources using strategic planning, architectures, and outcome-based performance measures to achieve a mission capability (CJCSI 8410.01, Warfighting Mission Area Information Technology Portfolio Management and Net-Centric Data Sharing). (DoDD 8115.01).

Lead Command —A type of MAJCOM that consolidates responsibilities for a particular function in a single MAJCOM, supporting the entire AF as applicable. (AFI 38-101).

Mission Area Roadmap—A plan which guides the implementation of capabilities across a Mission Area. (DoDD 8115.02).

National Security System (NSS)—Any information system (including any telecommunications system) used or operated by an agency or by a contractor of an agency, or other organization on behalf of an agency, the function, operation, or use of which involves intelligence activities; involves cryptologic activities related to national security; involves command and control of military forces; involves equipment that is an integral part of a weapon or weapons system; or is critical to the direct fulfillment of military or intelligence missions. (40 USC 11103. See also NIST SP 800-59).

Operational Baseline (OB)—The Operational Baseline is the set of components of the AF IT infrastructure that specifies the exact laydown and configurations of hardware and software within all facilities in the AF infrastructure topology and provide the required warfighter capabilities and performance.

Platform Information Technology (PIT) — A special purpose system which employs computing resources (i.e., hardware, firmware, and optionally software) that are physically embedded in, dedicated to, or essential in real time to the mission performance. It only performs (i.e., is dedicated to) the information processing assigned to it by its hosting special purpose system (this is not for core services). Examples include, but are not limited to: SCADA type systems, training simulators, diagnostic test and maintenance equipment. (AFI 33-210).

Target Baseline (TB)—The Target Baseline specifies the standards, protocols, guidelines and implementation constraints for the future state of the AFIN Infrastructure. It is used to inform the development of the implementation baseline. The Target Baseline is thoroughly documented and continually updated based upon emerging industry standards and the evolving AFEA.

Warfighting Integration—Ensuring information interoperability and compatibility of warfighting capabilities (e.g., people, processes, and technology) across the Air Force service core functions and within joint capability areas.

Warfighting Mission Area (WMA—)—The WMA provides life cycle oversight to applicable DoD Component and Combatant Commander IT investments (programs, systems, and initiatives). WMA IT investments support and enhance the Chairman of the Joint Chiefs of

Staff's joint warfighting priorities while supporting actions to create a net-centric distributed force, capable of full spectrum dominance through decision and information superiority. WMA IT investments ensure Combatant Commands can meet the Chairman of the Joint Chiefs of Staff's strategic challenges to win the war on terrorism, accelerate transformation, and strengthen joint warfighting through organizational agility, action and decision speed, collaboration, outreach, and professional development. (DoDI 8115.02).

Cybersecurity Titles Published by 4th Watch Publishing Co.

NIST SP 500-288 Specification for WS-Biometric Devices (WS-BD)
NIST SP 500-291 V2 NIST Cloud Computing Standards Roadmap
NIST SP 500-292 NIST Cloud Computing Reference Architecture
NIST SP 500-293 V1 & V2 US Government Cloud Computing Technology Roadmap
NIST SP 500-293 V3 US Government Cloud Computing Technology Roadmap
NIST SP 500-299 NIST Cloud Computing Security Reference Architecture
NIST SP 500-304 Data Format for the Interchange of Fingerprint, Facial & Other Biometric Information
NIST SP 800-12 R1 An Introduction to Information Security
NIST SP 800-16 R1 A Role-Based Model for Federal Information Technology/Cybersecurity Training
NIST SP 800-18 R1 Developing Security Plans for Federal Information Systems
NIST SP 800-22 R1a A Statistical Test Suite for Random and Pseudorandom Number Generators for Cryptographic Applications
NIST SP 800-30 Guide for Conducting Risk Assessments
NIST SP 800-31 Intrusion Detection Systems
NIST SP 800-32 Public Key Technology and the Federal PKI Infrastructure
NIST SP 800-34 R1 Contingency Planning Guide for Federal Information Systems
NIST SP 800-35 Guide to Information Technology Security Services
NIST SP 800-36 Guide to Selecting Information Technology Security Products
NIST SP 800-37 R2 Applying Risk Management Framework to Federal Information
NIST SP 800-38 Recommendation for Block Cipher Modes of Operation
NIST SP 800-38A Addendum Block Cipher Modes of Operation: Three Variants of Ciphertext Stealing for CBC Mode
NIST SP 800-38B Block Cipher Modes of Operation: The CMAC Mode for Authentication
NIST SP 800-38C Block Cipher Modes of Operation: The CCM Mode for Authentication and Confidentiality
NIST SP 800-38D Block Cipher Modes of Operation: Galois/Counter Mode (GCM) and GMAC
NIST SP 800-38E Block Cipher Modes of Operation: The XTS-AES Mode for Confidentiality on Storage Devices
NIST SP 800-38F Block Cipher Modes of Operation: Methods for Key Wrapping
NIST SP 800-38G Block Cipher Modes of Operation: Methods for Format-Preserving Encryption
NIST SP 800-39 Managing Information Security Risk
NIST SP 800-40 R3 Guide to Enterprise Patch Management Technologies
NIST SP 800-41 Guidelines on Firewalls and Firewall Policy
NIST SP 800-44 V2 Guidelines on Securing Public Web Servers
NIST SP 800-45 V2 Guidelines on Electronic Mail Security
NIST SP 800-46 R2 Guide to Enterprise Telework, Remote Access, and Bring Your Own Device (BYOD) Security
NIST SP 800-47 Security Guide for Interconnecting Information Technology Systems
NIST SP 800-48 Guide to Securing Legacy IEEE 802.11 Wireless Networks
NIST SP 800-49 Federal S/MIME V3 Client Profile
NIST SP 800-50 Building an Information Technology Security Awareness and Training Program
NIST SP 800-52 R1 Guidelines for the Selection, Configuration, and Use of Transport Layer Security (TLS) Implementations
NIST SP 800-53 R5 Security and Privacy Controls for Information Systems and Organizations
NIST SP 800-53A R4 Assessing Security and Privacy Controls
NIST SP 800-54 Border Gateway Protocol Security
NIST SP 800-56A R3 Pair-Wise Key-Establishment Schemes Using Discrete Logarithm Cryptography
NIST SP 56B R 1 Recommendation for Pair-Wise Key-Establishment Schemes Using Integer Factorization Cryptography
NIST SP 800-56C R1 Recommendation for Key-Derivation Methods in Key-Establishment Schemes - Draft
NIST SP 800-57 R4 Recommendation for Key Management
NIST SP 800-58 Security Considerations for Voice Over IP Systems
NIST SP 800-60 Guide for Mapping Types of Information and Information Systems to Security Categories
NIST SP 800-61 R2 Computer Security Incident Handling Guide
NIST SP 800-63-3 Digital Identity Guidelines
NIST SP 800-63a Digital Identity Guidelines - Enrollment and Identity Proofing
NIST SP 800-63b Digital Identity Guidelines - Authentication and Lifecycle Management
NIST SP 800-63c Digital Identity Guidelines- Federation and Assertions
NIST SP 800-64 R2 Security Considerations in the System Development Life Cycle
NIST SP 800-66 Implementing the Health Insurance Portability and Accountability Act (HIPAA) Security Rule
NIST SP 800-67 R2 Recommendation for Triple Data Encryption Algorithm (TDEA) Block Cipher - Draft
NIST SP 800-70 R4 National Checklist Program for IT Products
NIST SP 800-72 Guidelines on PDA Forensics
NIST SP 800-73-4 Interfaces for Personal Identity Verification
NIST SP 800-76-2 Biometric Specifications for Personal Identity Verification
NIST SP 800-77 Guide to IPsec VPNs
NIST SP 800-79-2 Authorization of Personal Identity Verification Card Issuers (PCI) and Derived PIV Credential Issuers (DPCI)
NIST SP 800-81-2 Secure Domain Name System (DNS) Deployment Guide
NIST SP 800-82 R2 Guide to Industrial Control Systems (ICS) Security
NIST SP 800-83 Guide to Malware Incident Prevention and Handling for Desktops and Laptops
NIST SP 800-84 Guide to Test, Training, and Exercise Programs for IT Plans and Capabilities
NIST SP 800-85A-4 PIV Card Application and Middleware Interface Test Guidelines
NIST SP 800-85B-4 PIV Data Model Test Guidelines - Draft
NIST SP 800-86 Guide to Integrating Forensic Techniques into Incident Response

NIST SP 1800-4a & 4b Mobile Device Security: Cloud and Hybrid Builds
NIST SP 1800-4c Mobile Device Security: Cloud and Hybrid Builds
NIST SP 1800-5 IT Asset Management: Financial Services
NIST SP 1800-6 Domain Name Systems-Based Electronic Mail Security
NIST SP 1800-7 Situational Awareness for Electric Utilities
NIST SP 1800-8 Securing Wireless Infusion Pumps
NIST SP 1800-9a & 9b Access Rights Management for the Financial Services Sector
NIST SP 1800-9c Access Rights Management for the Financial Services Sector - How To Guide
NIST SP 1800-11a & 11b Data Integrity Recovering from Ransomware and Other Destructive Events
NIST SP 1800-11c Data Integrity Recovering from Ransomware and Other Destructive Events - How To Guide
NIST SP 1800-12 Derived Personal Identity Verification (PIV) Credentials
NISTIR 7298 R2 Glossary of Key Information Security Terms
NISTIR 7316 Assessment of Access Control Systems
NISTIR 7497 Security Architecture Design Process for Health Information Exchanges (HIEs)
NISTIR 7511 R4 V1.2 Security Content Automation Protocol (SCAP) Version 1.2 Validation Program Test Requirements
NISTIR 7628 R1 Vol 1 Guidelines for Smart Grid Cybersecurity - Architecture, and High-Level Requirements
NISTIR 7628 R1 Vol 2 Guidelines for Smart Grid Cybersecurity - Privacy and the Smart Grid
NISTIR 7628 R1 Vol 3 Guidelines for Smart Grid Cybersecurity - Supportive Analyses and References
NISTIR 7756 CAESARS Framework Extension: An Enterprise Continuous Monitoring Technical Refer
NISTIR 7788 Security Risk Analysis of Enterprise Networks Using Probabilistic Attack Graphs
NISTIR 7823 Advanced Metering Infrastructure Smart Meter Upgradeability Test Framework
NISTIR 7874 Guidelines for Access Control System Evaluation Metrics
NISTIR 7904 Trusted Geolocation in the Cloud: Proof of Concept Implementation
NISTIR 7924 Reference Certificate Policy
NISTIR 7987 Policy Machine: Features, Architecture, and Specification
NISTIR 8006 NIST Cloud Computing Forensic Science Challenges
NISTIR 8011 Vol 1 Automation Support for Security Control Assessments
NISTIR 8011 Vol 2 Automation Support for Security Control Assessments
NISTIR 8040 Measuring the Usability and Security of Permuted Passwords on Mobile Platforms
NISTIR 8053 De-Identification of Personal Information
NISTIR 8054 NSTIC Pilots: Catalyzing the Identity Ecosystem
NISTIR 8055 Derived Personal Identity Verification (PIV) Credentials (DPC) Proof of Concept Research
NISTIR 8060 Guidelines for the Creation of Interoperable Software Identification (SWID) Tags
NISTIR 8062 Introduction to Privacy Engineering and Risk Management in Federal Systems
NISTIR 8074 Vol 1 & Vol 2 Strategic U.S. Government Engagement in International Standardization to Achieve U.S. Objectives for Cybersecurity
NISTIR 8080 Usability and Security Considerations for Public Safety Mobile Authentication
NISTIR 8089 An Industrial Control System Cybersecurity Performance Testbed
NISTIR 8112 Attribute Metadata - Draft
NISTIR 8135 Identifying and Categorizing Data Types for Public Safety Mobile Applications
NISTIR 8138 Vulnerability Description Ontology (VDO)
NISTIR 8144 Assessing Threats to Mobile Devices & Infrastructure
NISTIR 8151 Dramatically Reducing Software Vulnerabilities
NISTIR 8170 The Cybersecurity Framework
NISTIR 8176 Security Assurance Requirements for Linux Application Container Deployments
NISTIR 8179 Criticality Analysis Process Model
NISTIR 8183 Cybersecurity Framework Manufacturing Profile
NISTIR 8192 Enhancing Resilience of the Internet and Communications Ecosystem
Whitepaper Cybersecurity Framework Manufacturing Profile
Whitepaper NIST Framework for Improving Critical Infrastructure Cybersecurity
Whitepaper Challenging Security Requirements for US Government Cloud Computing Adoption
FIPS PUBS 140-2 Security Requirements for Cryptographic Modules
FIPS PUBS 140-2 Annex A Approved Security Functions
FIPS PUBS 140-2 Annex B Approved Protection Profiles
FIPS PUBS 140-2 Annex C Approved Random Number Generators
FIPS PUBS 140-2 Annex D Approved Key Establishment Techniques
FIPS PUBS 180-4 Secure Hash Standard (SHS)
FIPS PUBS 186-4 Digital Signature Standard (DSS)
FIPS PUBS 197 Advanced Encryption Standard (AES)
FIPS PUBS 198-1 The Keyed-Hash Message Authentication Code (HMAC)
FIPS PUBS 199 Standards for Security Categorization of Federal Information and Information Systems
FIPS PUBS 200 Minimum Security Requirements for Federal Information and Information Systems
FIPS PUBS 201-2 Personal Identity Verification (PIV) of Federal Employees and Contractors
FIPS PUBS 202 SHA-3 Standard: Permutation-Based Hash and Extendable-Output Functions

DHS Study DHS Study on Mobile Device Security

OMB A-130 / FISMA OMB A-130/Federal Information Security Modernization Act
GAO Federal Information System Controls Audit Manual

DoD	
UFC 3-430-11	Boiler Control Systems
UFC 4-010-06	Cybersecurity of Facility-Related Control Systems
FC 4-141-05N	Navy and Marine Corps Industrial Control Systems Monitoring Stations
MIL-HDBK-232A	RED/BLACK Engineering-Installation Guidelines
MIL-HDBK 1195	Radio Frequency Shielded Enclosures
TM 5-601	Supervisory Control and Data Acquisition (SCADA) Systems for C4ISR Facilities
ESTCP	Facility-Related Control Systems Cybersecurity Guideline
ESTCP	Facility-Related Control Systems Ver 4.0
DoD	Self-Assessing Security Vulnerabilities & Risks of Industrial Controls
DoD	Program Manager's Guidebook for Integrating the Cybersecurity Risk Management Framework (RMF) into the System Acquisition Lifecycle
DoD	Advanced Cyber Industrial Control System Tactics, Techniques, and Procedures (ACI TTP)
DoD 4140.1	Supply Chain Materiel Management Procedures
AFI 17-2NAS	Network Attack System (NAS) Vol. 1, 2 & 3
AFI 17-2ACD	Air Force Cyberspace Defense (ACD) Vol. 1, 2 & 3
AFI 10-1703	Air Force Cyberspace Training Publications
AFPD 17-2	Air Force Cyberspace Operations
AFI 17-2CSCS	Air Force Cyberspace Security and Control System (CSCS) Vol. 1, 2 & 3